sound

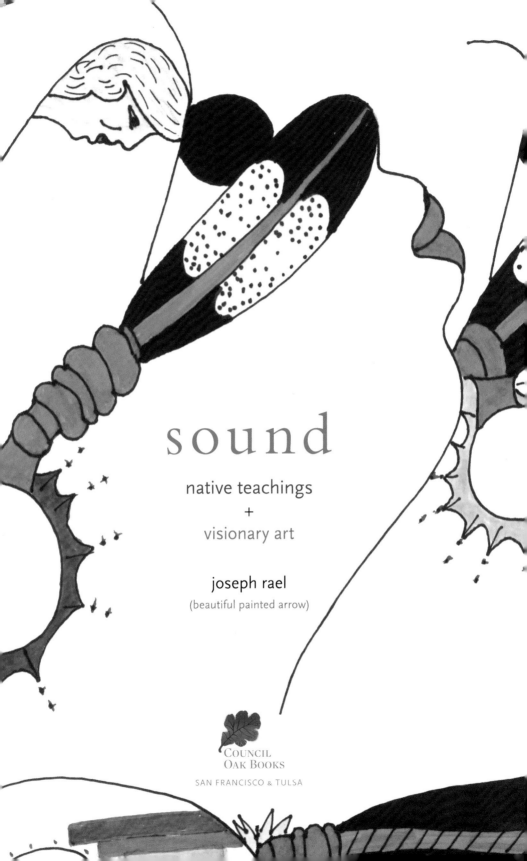

sound

native teachings
+
visionary art

joseph rael
(beautiful painted arrow)

COUNCIL
OAK BOOKS

SAN FRANCISCO & TULSA

New
Awareness
Old
Awareness

www.counciloakbooks.com

©2009 Joseph Rael. All rights reserved

Cover and interior artwork © 2009 by Joseph Rael
All rights reserved

Portions originally published in *The Way of Inspiration* ©1996
and in *Ceremonies of the Living Spirit* ©1998 by Joseph Rael

Audio online at josephrael.org © 1997 & 2009 by Joseph Rael
All rights reserved

First edition. First printing

LIBRARY OF CONGRESS CATALOGING-IN-PUBLICATION DATA
Rael, Joseph.
Sound : the native teachings & visionary art of Joseph Real
(Beautiful Painted Arrow) / Joseph Rael. -- 1st ed.
   p. cm.
ISBN 978-1-57178-186-4 (alk. paper)
1. Music--Religious aspects. 2. Dance--Religious aspects.
3. Sound--Religious aspects. 4. Rael, Joseph--Religion.
5. Rael, Joseph--Philosophy. I. Title.
BL605.R34 2009
299.7'840092--dc22

                                        2009018060

Printed in Canada

ISBN 978-1-57178-186-4

Cover and interior design by Carl Brune

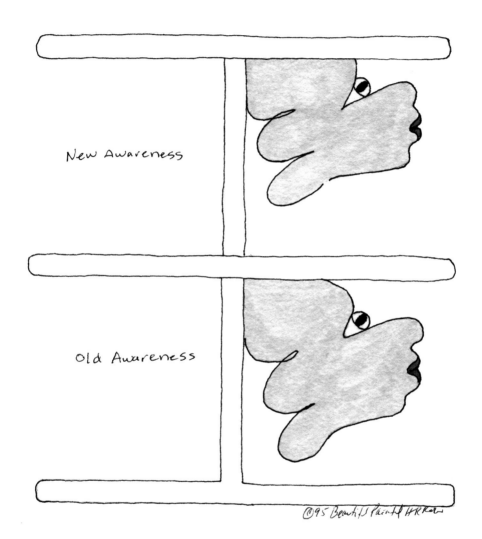

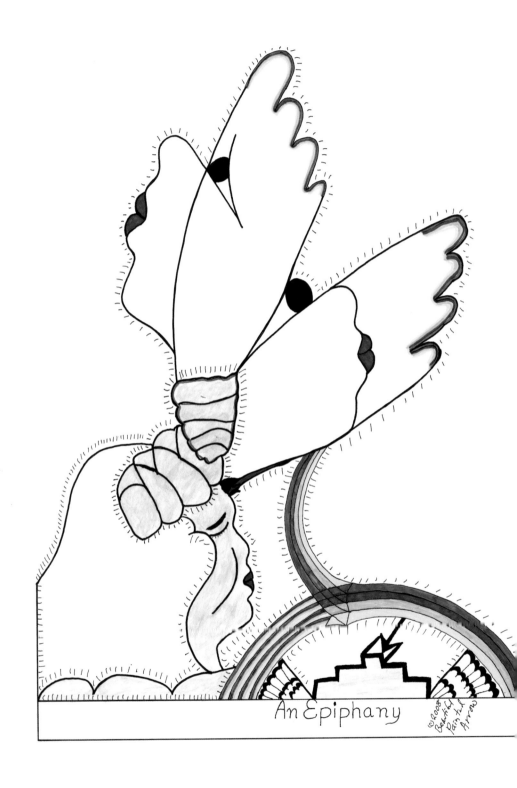

An Epiphany

©2008
Beautiful
Painted
Arrow

contents

An
Epiphany

moon mountain

Sun Rise mountain

Seekers of Divine Guidance

©2009
Joanne Bowlick
Painted Arrow

echo

In the beginning before time, before the cosmos is created, the people do not exist in physical forms, so this teaching is about how "the people," invisible ones, become the visible made ones.

— JOSEPH RAEL

We do not exist.

To understand this truth requires a transformation of one's way of understanding the cosmos. For most people, this does not come about through intellect so much as through absorption, in the same way a tree absorbs the elements of life through leaves and roots.

Life is breath, matter and movement. God's breath is black light and white light in dialog, and all of perceptual reality is vibration.

Modern physics teaches similar things of course, but I did not learn these truths from a study of physics. I received this knowledge in visions connected to teachings that were imparted to me in my grandfather's kiva at Picuris Pueblo more than sixty years ago. Everything observable and non-observable in this sphere of perceptual reality is the result of the breath of God, moving in the space-time continuum, creating matter, creating life.

All of my teachings tie into the reality that there is a Seer seeing everything. We call it God, the higher power, or whatever. It is simply the Vast Self seeing itself creating itself. We humans perceive ourselves and the world around us as solid objects, as flesh and bone, sitting on a padded chair, or on grass-covered earth. But all these things, the flesh, bones, chair, grass and earth, are artifacts of one great collective act of perceiving in which all beings participate. What we perceive as solid, having dimensions and colors and other properties, are really just pulses of energy moving or vibrating, each in its unique pattern, so as to interact with our patterns, to excite our senses and create patterns of perception.

Seekers
of Divine
Guidance

1

We are perceivers, and it is in our act of perceiving that vibrations become sounds, smells, feelings and colors. In our act of perceiving, things take form.

And thus, we do not exist. We, the perceivers, and all our organs of perception are patterns of movement. We pulse in and out of existence constantly. Of course we do not perceive our pulsing, for, at the instant we blink out of existence, we lose our power of perception. Our existence comes across to us as a continuum, but it is not. We are constantly flashing on and off, strobe-like, a drumbeat, returning to the silent void and then back again to this perceptual reality.

Another way to say this is that we are constantly being unmade and then remade. Each time we are unmade, each time we return to the void, we are changed in the remaking. In fact, it is only in those instants of non-being that we have the power to change. It is only when we are unmade and remade that the new thing can come into this perceptual reality. Change is only possible because we really are not the solid beings in continuous existence that we think we are.

God's breath is the power, the energy of matter in movement. Because of this on–off-on–off pulsation, we become matter. We matter because we move. We move because God breathes. On the one hand, we each move in patterns unique to ourselves, but on the other hand, we do not exist at all: we are nothing.

The teachings collected here under the title *Sound* are all based on one central fact: The true basis for Universal Intelligence is sound. Out of sound comes everything.

To me the body (including the feelings) represents the land, the Vast Self. The thought and the brain are what come out of the Vast Self, but then the brain sits up there on its throne and wants to run things, control things. That is fine for a while, but eventually it has to understand that it is not independent and it has to merge and come together in the vastness of the Vast Self in order to touch reality.

The rational mind tells us that whatever it cannot understand is not real, and that misconception is what separates

josephrael.org/
bmm.mp3

echo

2

us from God. To express these truths in writing, in a book, puts me in the position of using a rational, linear form of communication to convey a belief system that is profoundly non-linear, and non-rational, but is more truly true.

I suggest that you read this book in the same way you would listen to music. If you can approach this experience with all your doors of perception wide open, perhaps the words and images here might seep into your being through the spaces of nonbeing, and you will be forever changed.

Enter this book of my teachings as if you were climbing down into a kiva for sacred ceremony. Do not come to be instructed. Come to be initiated.

e c h o

Blessing for all life

the people and the land

One day in the spring of the year during the mid 1940s, while we were plowing our fields at Picuris Pueblo in north central New Mexico, I came upon an understanding, and that understanding was that the spoken English language I was learning at the local day school and the Tiwa language that was spoken at our pueblo were both connections to the land.

josephrael.org/
nature.mp3

The Picuris Pueblo of that era was a traditional hunting, gathering and farming society. All the food we ate came from the land upon which we also lived. When we at Picuris Pueblo were living off the land-base, we were tending, caretaking, and nurturing ourselves. As we plowed and planted the land each spring, we were revitalizing and empowering ourselves. As we tended the crops, we were developing our own individual strengths. And as we harvested and prepared and ate the food, we were completing the circle, taking into ourselves the energy we had poured into the growing and hunting and gathering of our food.

Blessings
for all life

I saw the connection that all the natural sounds, the vibrations of nature that were in the spoken English or spoken Tiwa languages, also vibrated in the land and sky. The sound of winds blowing beyond the branches of trees, the sound vibrations of animals communing with their environs, the whispering of the soil as a plant awakens from the seed, these were all encoded in the spoken Tiwa or English word, and in order to awaken them in ourselves, we were to farm the land. I had the revelation that the original ideas that make up our human bodies were vibrations instilled in matter, instilled in soil and seed and grain.

5

The land on which we live is the means by which we are making ourselves anew. At Picuris our home was the "loving-self place" and homegrown food from our vegetable gardens, fruit trees, wild berries and roots were all composed of the energies of this loving-self place. Consequently when we were planting the land at Picuris, we were planting, in a real sense, ourselves, renewing our beingness. Planting the fields was an important part of our existence because it was the beginning of the growing cycle. Our destinies at the planting time of the year were to recreate the cosmos annually.

The food that we harvested and that we ate was spiritual food for the sustenance of the Infinite Self. It encoded the essence of spiritual law. We were the children of the soil and the soil was made up of all things remembered, all the plants and animals and people who had lived and eaten and planted there before us were part of the humus that produced the food we ate, and all our history and tradition was there in its vibrations. Our elders instilled in us the knowledge that links with the past were our bonds to the future. Thus the land brought us understanding, simply because we were walking on it, eating from it, and its energies had become us. The land under us, and we above it, were being nurtured as well by the above sky-mind, bonding itself to us and then to the lands beneath us.

josephrael.org/
land.mp3

The revelation was larger still and it was that we could be playing out any role at any time on the stage of the local community. The family, the extended family and other members of the community united to work the land together.

The family was made up of fathers, mothers, brothers, sisters, aunts, uncles, grandmothers, grandfathers, and so forth. The words for each of these roles were made up of sounds, each of which has a meaning. For instance, the eldest brother was *pah-pah* in the Tiwa language. The *ah* carries the meaning "to wash." The consonant sound "p" is the sound of the beating heart. These sounds reminded us of how, with each pulse, the physical heart sent out blood to irrigate and purify all parts of the body. Thus, whenever a person saw his elder brother coming toward him in the village and said the word "pah-pah," that person was honoring the brother with the name of "the pulsating heart that purifies." Indeed, at the center of the village is a tall wooden pole that symbolizes the heart of the village, the place from which purifying energy goes out in a circle and to which it returns again. Each August we have a ceremony in which the pole is replaced with a new one, and young men climb the new pole in a celebration of brotherly love.

The other designations were:

Father — acting of goodness
Mother — key to purity
Little Brother — light of the myth
Sister — abundance
Little Sister — light of many stories
Aunt — purity that is carrying infinity
Uncle — seed planted
Grandmother — elder creator
Grandfather — elder creator

These names were those of the ones who came in the beginning as the action of goodness (Father), the key to purity (Mother), the washing heart (Brother), the light of the myth (Little Brother), the abundance beyond abundance (Sister), the light of many stories (Little Sister), the purity that is carrying infinity (Aunt), the planted seed (Uncle), and the elder creators (Grandmother and Grandfather). In this way our shared language teaches us to respect each of our relatives and encourages us to harmonize our relationships with each other.

I learned by observing the rhythms of the land, paying attention to the early spring times and the birth of tiny new grass blades poking through the fresh soil of the furrows just plowed. Every spring I grew in knowledge of the Divine Woman as I followed my father behind the horse-drawn plow. We plowed and we planted. In the dropping of the corn kernels we created the resonance of woman. So it was in each season; I learned by being part of something beyond myself, part of the rhythmic beauty of the ever-changing land.

In the wintertime when earth was sleeping, we were taught by Myth Maker and Storyteller that we were manifestations of

Core of the Earth

MotherEarth and the flowering of Life

2005
© Beautiful Painted Arrow

the purifying light and that we came into being through the awareness of the purifying heart.

What we practice, what patterns we repeat, eventually we become. When we sustain ourselves through the energies of the land, there is a synchronicity between land and our physical and spiritual selves and with each other. Then we are in good health. When we don't sustain ourselves in this synchronicity with the land, we will tend to polarize.

After I had been gone from Picuris Pueblo for 36 years, from "the ranch," as we called our home at the pueblo, on my return, at the precise moment I entered the fence line, walking toward our ranch house, I sensed an energy similar in vibration to my own physical energy. The knowingness that I had just received was that the land and I were the same—that we shared the same sensitivity. I had rediscovered myself! The land and I still carried the same resonating vibration that had been given to me in my formative years. There was no other way to explain this phenomenon but to say that the foods I had eaten from it and my having walked on it and lived on it through my growing up years had formed my mental, emotional, physical and spiritual resonance. Eating the food from the land base of our local community had given me my personal orientation.

The mythic tradition made of memory teaches that the flower garden is the earth and that one of the life forms on it is the human. As a group, humans are co-creators. At Picuris the earth was seen as the "ever-blooming flower" because it was stuck at the flowering stage of the life cycle. "It will remain at the blooming stage until we worship it through work, which can take us beyond the physical laws," the elder said to me fifty years ago at Picuris Pueblo. "Life will never ripen and bear fruit, but will always remain as a flower" unless we go beyond it to the future. We can live both the flowering and the fruit by living the land's vibration in our moments lived well in the here and now.

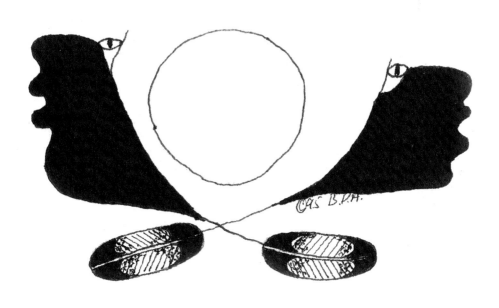

sound at the beginning

The mystery of life is very simple, so simple that anybody can understand it. The truth is this: Sound is the basis for all that is.

Everything comes out of sound, and sound comes out of vibration. Sound was the deity that first said "yes" to life. Before that there was no life. Once Sound said "yes" to life, then everything began to flow out of that sound. And that sound was the sound of silence. Out of that sound of silence came the first go-ahead to life. Then consciousness began to flow. It began to flow in the same way as the blood begins to flow in the human body.

That sound is what created time. Time is the power to crystallize awareness so that manifestation can find placement. Time found space and there was a marriage of the two. Before that nothing had a place, nothing knew where it was supposed to be. Once we had sound, out of sound came everything.

I have spent fifty years trying to teach this truth: *Sound is powerful*. It is actually the polarities coming together, one hitting the other, like two hands clapping. Sounds are powers. Language is power. The power is not primarily in the intellectual concepts language is expressing, but in the very sounds of the words. Conceptualization is not the basis for Universal Intelligence; the true basis for Universal Intelligence is sound.

If you go back to the original sound it will awaken the archetypal vibrations in you. We are like the top of the carrot. We need to go back down to the root, the very tip. That is where the Circle of Light is. It exists at the subatomic level. We have to go down to it and bring whatever is there up to higher and higher levels of consciousness.

The goal of these mystery teachings is to put us in touch with the cosmos that we live in and the other universes that exist alongside our universe. If we are going to go back to the

the voice
of silence

sound
at
the
beginning

11

true mystery of life, we have to educate ourselves about sound.

Everything has a sound. Drag an object and it says "dragging." The sound of knocking creates the god—or archetype—of knocking. The floor has the power of flooring. Everything is a power; it embodies an archetype. We are living in the midst of the mystery of life, but we are living in ignorance. We don't know that the room we are in is a holy chapel; the floor, the walls, and the ceiling are holy vibrations.

My vision is that through sound we will bring about peace and other important vibrations. Sound can teach us a way to create without destruction.

When we left our genesis, moved away from the sound that created us, we left behind some of the powers we started with. We should have taken all our possibilities with us. We lost our powers and have replaced them with technologies. When we lost the potentials we originally had and began to develop technologies, we began to use the natural resources in order to replace those lost powers. We need get those original powers back. We can do that by contacting our relatives in the other realities, by going back and listening to the language of the land.

josephrael.org/
origins.mp3

There is a language of the land and it has the vibration of those original sounds that created us. When you hear the language of the land, you will know that language, because all humanity comes from sound. First of all, we are the land and then after that we are whatever we make of ourselves. English and other modern languages are derivatives that have gotten away from those original sounds. English is a language of technology. Indigenous languages that have been used for millennia by people living close to the land carry the original vibration of the language of the land.

sound
at
the
beginning

Tiwa, the language I learned at Picuris Pueblo when I was a child, isn't a "word language," it is a sound language. It is an example of the language of the land. It came not from the people's desire to communicate, but from their desire to stay as close as possible to Creator's gift of manifestation—life. To stay as close as possible to that life in this realm was to sound whatever happened to exist at the moment. If you were standing, for instance, and you could get in touch with how standing sounds, then you couldn't possibly stray too far from wisdom: physical wisdom, or intellectual wisdom, or emotional wisdom, or spiritual wisdom.

Instilled in the ancient metaphoric language of the Tiwa are many answers. I have been studying the Picuris Tiwa for over fifty years, using art to discover revelation and reading the Tiwa texts. Spirituality is packed inside the Tiwa language of the land. The power of Spirit is in the sounds.

sound
at
the
beginning

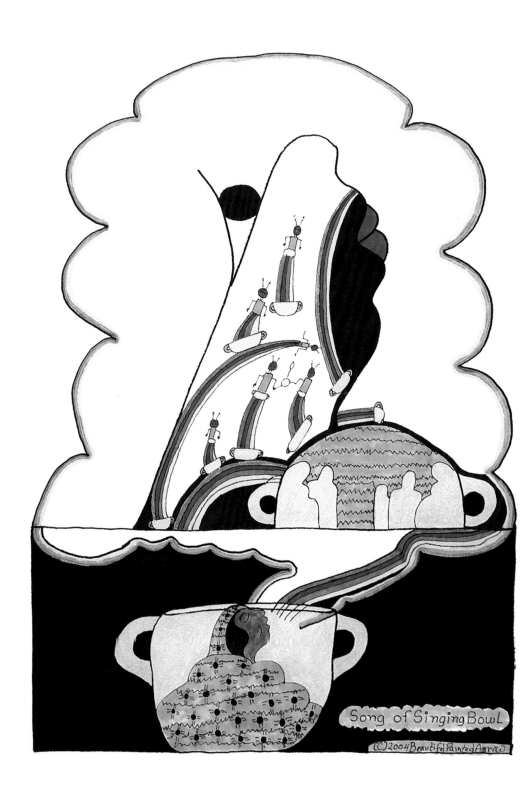

Song of Singing Bowl

©2004 Beautiful Painted Arrow

using sound

Once upon a time a bowl was singing, and they say the song came out of Singing Bowl. She came to bring the voice sound of language to all creations. No one knows how long ago it was. They just remember that she made time from song, and time became the circle and the square and the spaces inside the lines of the circle and the lines inside the square. She made them to be invisible so she could fill them with the Intelligence of Knowing.

When I was about eight, I was learning three languages simultaneously: Spanish, English, and Tiwa, the language of Picuris Pueblo. Until that time I had only spoken Ute. Learning these languages made me aware of the differences among languages and the similarities. I began to understand the power of all language.

Song of Singing Bowl

In order to learn the languages, I had to listen very carefully to the sounds. As I vocalized the sounds and meditated on them, I came to the realization that sounds, especially vowel sounds, are the vibrations of principal ideas encoded in the human gene pool. Words made from these sounds will carry within them the principal ideas that are the same, no matter what language a person is speaking.

Language always fascinated me; I wanted to know what makes life the way it is. I wanted to know where the energies were before creation. Where did they come from? Before creation, we had all the constituent parts that make up the essence of beingness.

Eventually, I developed an understanding of the principal ideas behind each of the five vowel sounds:

> **A** = purification
>
> **E** = placement

I = awareness

O = childlike innocence

U = carrying

Using this knowledge, I can go beyond the surface meaning of a word in Tiwa or Spanish or English or whatever language, to discover the principal ideas with which it is connected. I can chant the vowel sounds in a word like "table" or "walking" and connect on a vibratory level with the principal ideas that created those forms.

josephrael.org/
AEIOU.mp3

josephrael.org/
ahhh.mp3

josephrael.org/
ehh.mp3

josephrael.org/
ohh.mp3

josephrael.org/
iii.mp3

josephrael.org/
uuu.mp3

Make a Song

One way to awaken the archetypal vibrations within yourself is to create your own song using the ancient vibrations of the Language of the Land, the pure vowel sounds of "ahh, eh, iii, ooh, uuu."

We came out of song, so when we go back to song we expand those original vibrations in ourselves. When you create your own chant with the pure vowel sounds, the sounds will teach you. How do you feel with each vibration? Is there a sound that wants to come forward? Create your song around that sound.

using
sound

Sound Healing for Humans

To bring about wellness, we sing the sound of the area of the human body that needs healing. For example, to heal an injured hand, we make the sound of the hand by chanting the word for "hand" in Tiwa, "mah-neh-neh." However, the real-real reason we are also chanting the hand sound is so that the rest of the physical body of the patient can come to its aid.

The healer instructs the patient to chant the hand sound quietly until the patient's mind senses the hand sound everywhere in the physical body.

This is the use of holistic healing sound. Further, because the patient speaks and writes English, the world "hand" can be used as a chant sound along with the visualization of the injured hand being healed. In time the patient will sense the vibration of the hand sound all over his/her physical body, and the body's healing powers will come to help heal the injury. The person will be healed by just sensing and visualizing the sounds.

Here is a second method: In this method, the doctor instructs the patient to visualize and chant the sound the vowel letter in the written word hand — the "a" sound or "aah" sound. In the same way, vowel sounds can be chanted for other parts of the human body.

Health providers and doctors who have tried the sound method have been quite successful. (They also choose not to be recorded.) You may want to include other sounds like heart, legs, skin, etc.

Human Anatomy

Brain=*aah-ii*
Eye=*eh-eh*
Facial Nerve=*aah-ii-aah*
Spine=*ii-eh*
Ribs=*ii*
Lung=*uu*
Spleen=*eh-eh*
Stomach=*ooh-aah*
Kidney=*ii-eh-ii*
Rectum=*eh-uu*
Femoral Artery=*eh-ooh-aah/
    aah-eh-ii*
Femur=*eh-uu*
Patella/Knee bone=*aah-eh-aah*
Tibia (just below the knee-
    bone)=*ii-ii-aah*
Feet/Ankles=*ii-ii/aah-eh*

Sky Father covers Earth Mother with "SPIRIT" Leaves for new trees just planted after the summer fires.

© 2008 Beautiful Painted Arrow

sound and the breath of god

n the beginning, according to the creation story, there was nothing. All was complete blankness. This nothingness wanted to bring itself into awareness, to know itself.

josephrael.org/
beginning.mp3

josephrael.org/
breath.mp3

Then, life was created by *Wah-mah-chi*, which is the Tiwa name for God, and means breath, matter, and movement. The breath is the inspiration in matter that brings all concreteness, or form, into existence via movement. Really only one thing exists, and that is the breath of God in a state of movement creating the vibration of matter.

When the Supreme Being breathed into the space of nothing, this created intent. This intent was divine calling, divine longing, creating matter in movement toward a particular direction. The word for "intent" in Tiwa is *poh-cheh*. *Poh* is "blowing breath" and *cheh* means eyes. *Poh-cheh* then, literally means "Blowing breath with eyes that see." With intent, or *poh-cheh*, perceptual reality was created.

Sky father covers Earth Mother with SPIRIT Leaves

In this creation time, the Great Mystery breathed into this nothingness and created the intent, the blowing breath with eyes that see, or perceptual reality. The intent was an integral part of heart. There was, then, the heart center, what we would know later as truth. And this heart center was connected to purity, and this purity was connected to beauty, and this beauty would bond all things.

As breath came into this space of nothingness, there was a mist like a white cloud, created by the tears of joy of the breath. The blowing breath with eyes to see how it was creating was now streaming with tears — rivers of consciousness. The water then began to fall onto the Earth. The Tiwa storyteller tells us that this first rainfall was the light coming from God. As it descended, it went down through endless space until it reached and touched the first essence of matter. Then matter and spirit began to create all of the eternities, and one of those eternities would be ours.

At that beginning, the land and the people and the sky were different manifestations of metaphor alongside experience. For every experience that was occurring, there was a metaphor to substantiate it.

This is how sound and imagery create physical form, matter. Without imagery and sound, matter cannot be created. Sound is the first phenomenon. In Tiwa, *poh* means blowing breath, and it also means sound. *Poh* also means the circle of the medicine wheel. Thus, sound and the medicine wheel are synonymous. In Tiwa sound is a "wheel of sound." Why? Because sound — all sound — is always at the center of the wheel (medicine circle) when a sound is first heard. It is said that sound has a physical character, a mental character, an emotional character, and a spiritual character.

Imagery came after sound. First was *poh*, then came imagery to fill in the *poh*, the first circle of light. Imagery is the combination of a number of essences that came together from the Vast Infinite Self in the very earliest moments of creation to form the stream of consciousness inside the circle of life, or medicine wheel. Those essences included awareness, manifestation, purity, goodness, relativity, radiance, and the capacity of transcendence.

Relativity is placement, and it is our connectedness with all things. Radiance is that essence that gives us our highs and lows.

Without imagery, matter could not be created. To make matter required movement of awareness in the play of the essences of purity, goodness, relativity, radiance, transcendence, or combinations of these. *I-ma-ge-ry*. The sound that it makes tells what it means: "To create while keeping a close watch over what is created, once it is given birth, so that life may know itself."

I now see this creation as a continual process, an evolution of consciousness that results from the interplay between the realm of pure ideas and the material realm. It is like a continual exchange of breath. Life energy (*waaa*), or inspiration, descends into the medicine wheel from the realm of pure ideas.

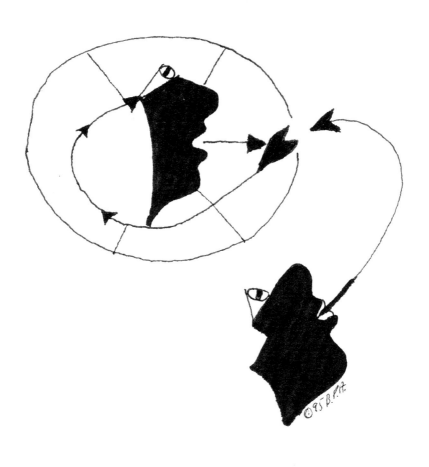

The infinite vast self

Consciousness always moves in circles. Apparently that is how life lives inside the cycles of time. Time travels together with the living essence of life in which, over cyclical time, everything becomes its opposite. At birth, humans are in the vibration of childlike innocence and at old age humans again become childlike. Over time, "what goes around comes around."

All of life moves in circles. All we have to do is look around us and see how life is a circle. Today, this is how I understand life. In a vision in the 1980s at a Sun Dance I saw how creation happens, and it is happening all the time.

Oneness is the breath (celestial winds) as blowing dark energy, which then creates matter (duality), and it in turn creates *movement* or perception. Hence, *breath, matter and movement*. Without movement we would not have the abilities for growth, change and our abilities to see with our eyes. Perception requires movement. Life has to step back to see itself. Life is sacred because it is always thinking, talking, living as Divine Presence.

Images of creation come to me from the ceremonies of my people. My Tiwa people hold a festival day each August 10 at Picuris Pueblo, which climaxes with the climbing of a pole. Before the day begins, a pole about twenty-five feet tall has been cut from a tree on the mountain, brought down, and set up in the center of the pueblo. This pole becomes the heart-center of the village. At the top of this pole are tied a sheep, a basket of bread, and a watermelon. After a day of sacred ceremonies, feasting, running, and dancing, clown dancers emerge from the kiva and try to climb the pole. Climbing the pole is not easy and only the strongest men can do it. If no one were able to do it, we believe our village would die. Every year of our existence someone has come forth to climb the pole, and eventually, one of the clowns or another young man from the pueblo succeeds in getting to the top. When he does, he unties the sheep, the bread, and the watermelon, and brings them down to the people in the village.

Among my Southern Ute people, an annual sun dance

sound
and
the
breath
of
god

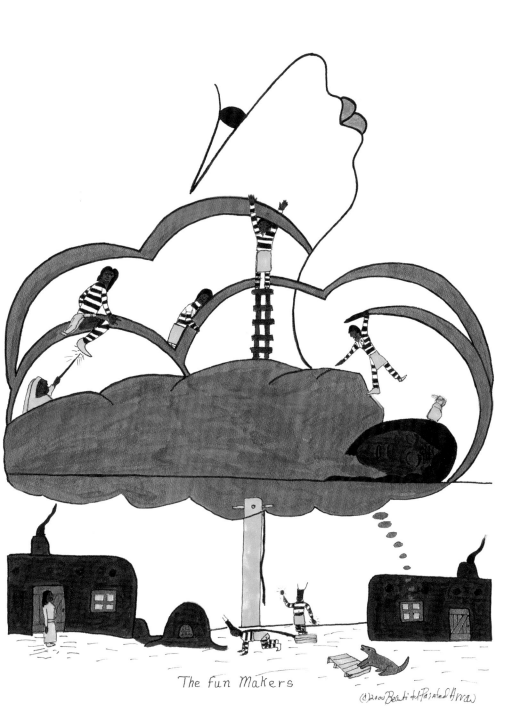

The Fun Makers

is held during which people who are fasting from food and water dance back and forth to the sun dance pole (made from a tree which was cut and placed in the middle of the sun dance circle). The sun dance circle is circumscribed by trees and represents the medicine wheel.

When I saw the clowns climbing up and down the pole at Picuris, I understood creation as a flash of new inspiration that was being brought to the Earth from a higher plane. And when I took part in the Ute sun dance I saw inspiration happening as a pulse of light radiating out from the heart center and then coming back in, bringing with it new energies for the next stage of human development. A pulse is a wave of light that is made of sound energy (vibration). In the Tiwa language, the word for "people" also means "vibration." The people feed on this new inspiration, the vibration changes, and consciousness is changed, just as, at Picuris and the Southern Ute Sun dance, a new pole replaces the old one each year.

The pole climb and the sun dance pole are the Indians' way to recreate how perceptual reality comes into being. These ceremonies re-enact how life is perpetually in a state of creativity. Of course, there is no "up-and-down" or "out-and-back-in" continuum in reality. We create these metaphors here in order to give purity, placement, awareness, innocence and carrying a structure. Only when these are ordered in a linear structure, oriented in time, can we perceive that which cannot be seen outside space and time.

It gives me great inner peace to search for the beauty in languages. A single word means many things, like the energy it carries and the intention for it. My meditation on the word leads me many times to new mystical revelations.

Here is an example. When I write about the Sun Dance ceremonies or Picuris Pueblo ceremonies or teachings, I am talking about inner meaning of the ideas or concepts in the dance forms, and not the process that happens.

Someone once said long ago, "there are no secrets under the sun."

Light energy is what empowers matter. Notice that light begins with the letter "L" ("El") — the name for God in many ancient languages. In the word light is God-ness. God is breath, matter and movement.

Sound light awakens matter into movement. Sound light is one single point of light, likened to a dot of light, that has a mental, emotional, physical and spiritual dimension. It is the seed of all that is. It is the medicine wheel.

The medicine wheel is the basic structure, or the essential metaphor, for all that is. Picture a medicine wheel, a circle divided into four parts. Think of the segments as winter in the north quadrant, spring in the east, summer in the south and autumn in the west. There is a line between winter and spring, showing the equinox where winter ends and spring begins. Exactly at that line is an opening that allows, and in fact demands, for new ideas to enter. Right at the line between winter and spring, new ideas enter via a slice of light into the medicine wheel. These lines between the seasons represent gates or doorways. Among my people, it is believed that there are gatekeepers. These gatekeepers are referred to as grandmothers or grandfathers — or, in Tiwa, as mother-father beings. Their responsibility is to let in the new ideas or to refuse their entry. At this precise point immediately after entry, *chaa-ched* happens. *Chaa* means the here-and-now. *Chaa* creates presentness in linear time. In the word *chaa-ched*, the *ched* means that which is perceptive. Before *ched* we do not have cognition because we cannot perceive. *Ched* is the vibration of perception.

Cha creates a place for an idea to appear and be rooted — to display its wares —while *ched* assigns the perceptual dimension of that which is coming into being.

Tie-eh-neh means "the people," and "the people" are vibrations. Vibration is energy, and we know that energy is electrons and quarks that make up atoms and molecules. Molecules are those vibrations that are actively engaged in the essence of doing. There is a movement going on.

Movement is what gives us the possibility of perception.

josephrael.org/
light.mp3

sound
and
the
breath
of
god

The Grand fathers

©2005 Joseph Beautiful PaintedArrow

Therefore, we exist in perceptual reality because of the dialog between time and space. Time is dragging along space. We say *"toh-peh"* which means to be moving forward. When you are moving forward you are opening a doorway into the unknown.

Time is pulling on us. This is because time has the capacity of crystallizing awareness so that it is manifest in placement. Time is the pulling force of manifestation.

And space is pushing us along.

Space bends time because space and light are in an interaction. I call it a dance. Light is coming from one star and passes another star. As it goes by, the next star bends it in – calls it—because of the space that the light is coming from. Scientists say that that is the gravitational pull of that star. The star pulls that light in … calls it. That is why I say there is a dance between space and light.

That light energy is material, but it also contains the spiritual. The light contains the essential ingredients for epiphanies and insights and the power for supernatural perception. Out of supernatural perception, then, comes ordinary perception.

Black light and white light ≈ Life was created with breath. When I breathe out, you hear the sound "hhhhhoooooow." That is the sound for the black light, which physicists call dark energy. The indigenous Americans who still speak the language of the land call it dark light or night light. Thus, dark energy is referred to as "hhhhhoooooow" (but the Tiwa–speakers put a "ney-ney" at the end of it, which means "that which is"). *Hhhhhhooooow-neh-neh* means "that which is the black light."

Since time was, the dark light was always here and so was the white light. There has been a dialog between the black light and the white light since before time was and it has always been here. That dark light is in each and every one of us, it is in this room, it is in the space in this room, it is in the space in the walls of this house, it is in the space outside. It is in our bodies. It is everywhere.

sound
and
the
breath
of
god

Physicists tell us that black light, or dark energy, is pushing everything farther and farther apart. When there is separation between you and a friend or loved one, it is an aspect of the tendency of the dark light in you to push away. The white light is in you, too, and its tendency is to bring in and incorporate. That dialog is the only thing that really exists. That is what causes the struggle within us. In our decision-making processes, really what we are dealing with is what the dark light and the white light are doing. In our perceptual reality, it looks like our particular struggles or life dramas, but really all there is is that dialog between dark light and white light.

The essences of the *ahh, eh, iii, ohh,* and *uu,* or purity, placement, awareness, childlike innocence and carrying, are really all part of the struggle or dance between the black light that is pushing things apart and the white light that is bringing things together.

The term "black light" doesn't refer to evil energy. The culture I come from teaches that there is no hell. There is only the dialog between night and day. We are "in the dark" and then all of sudden we have knowing and we are in the light.

Black light, or the dark light of the night times, is light that is so very, very pure that it cannot hold any of the colors of the rainbow. Black light is purer than white light. White light contains all the colors and allows us to see. Being enlightened with the white light, we then have connection to the knowledge that is stored in the blackness. All the potential is in the black light and the realization or materialization is seen in the white light, so those two have always been in an eternal level of dialog. What we experience as perceptual reality is the result of the dialog between the black light and the white light.

Drinking Light ≈ The soul in metaphor is the process of drinking light. Light is universal intelligence and love, and it cannot be stuck in the dark. When the soul does not drink light it begins to dry up. Loneliness and separation are the results of the soul's lacking nurturing, so there must be a continuous process to connect a soul to this flow of light or love out of which comes

Rainbow man
and rainbow
woman make
first Double
Rainbow on
Turtle Island

sound
and
the
breath
of
god

28

Rainbow man and rainbow woman make first Double Rainbow on Turtle Island

(C) Joseph Beautiful Painted Arrow

genuine fulfillment. The soul knows it is loved and cared for, and all it must do then is stay in touch with light-filled creativity. It wants to create perceptions that are full of light.

I think this is what the sound peace chambers are about. In 1984, I received the vision to build circular chambers where people chant together to bring about peace. Now over fifty such chambers have been built all around the world. They came into existence at this time to remind us, even if we never chant in them at all, that there is a concrete form where there is more going on than we can ever understand, here and now in the physical plane, to connect us to the spiritual plane.

About three months after I got the original idea to build the sound peace chambers, I had another vision. I was taken out of my body and brought before a ring of elders, who asked: "Why haven't you started building those peace chambers?" I said that it was because I couldn't find a place to build them. Next thing I knew there was a ring that came down from the heavens, showing me to build the first one next to my own trailer house in Bernalillo. And then a second ring came down, and there was an angel holding a little child. The angel placed the child on the Earth in the center of the circle of light. Then I heard the angel's voice say: "This child is for you to raise." I was supposed to be the foster father for it. It was like an idea that had come down.

Up and down are a metaphor for receiving something and giving back oneself. That is what is going on with ascending and descending light: giving and receiving at the same time. So what we have here is a new vibration given to the Earth. The Earth is a symbol of the Infinite Self, the Vast Self; that is what the soil is. And the grass is ancientness.

So, the child was given to the Earth. A few months later I was doing some lectures in Marin County, California. There was an educational institute, right on the cliffs, for the Sufis order, and I did a sweat lodge there, during which I had a visionary experience. In the vision, three men appeared. They jumped off the cliff and their force drove me out of my body, and pulled me. All three dove into the water, there were three white splashes, and I was falling; I was nothing but light.

Next thing, I was in the corridor, like an underground tunnel, and the last one of the three was in front of me and was pulling me along. He looked like a man with shoulder-length blond hair, but also looked like a fish, a green fish. Perhaps he was a merman. I saw him come into the light, and then, when I looked, I was in a big cave, and there was no water.

I saw a beautiful being sitting on a glowing throne studded with emeralds and diamonds. He had a cape that was blue and an almost childlike face, a baby's face. There was a pink color, very pleasant, very calm, very beautiful, and he put a light in front of him that looked like a blue teardrop.

He communicated with me telepathically, saying, "I want you to go back, and on the seventh of April I want you to build a fire in the chamber. It is for the purification of the oceans." I knew that he meant physical oceans, and that he also meant the cosmic ocean. And he said the light of the fire needed to be reflected against the wall of the chamber.

So then I went back and did the fire ceremony. In a flash of light I had been given all the details for the ceremony. In the vision, the steps were included, and it turned out that the logs for the fire were to be laid out like a tic-tac-toe grid.

So I started doing fire ceremonies every month on the seventh, and as other peace chambers were built, I instructed the people to do the ceremonies too, every month on the seventh, so that when April came around they wouldn't forget. Later I learned that the Greeks used to honor Oceanus on April 7 by making a fire. Maybe the being in the ocean was Oceanus or a manifestation of him. Oceanus is the metaphor for the birth of new ideas—babies. When we talk about the birth of babies, we are not just talking about the physical two-legged ones. We are talking about childhood in any dimension, as an idiom, an energy. Oceanus came to plant something new on the planet. I took his ceremony and I built fire, and with that fire he was there.

Fire is the seed in the womb-like peace chambers. Birth is reflected off the walls from the center of the room.

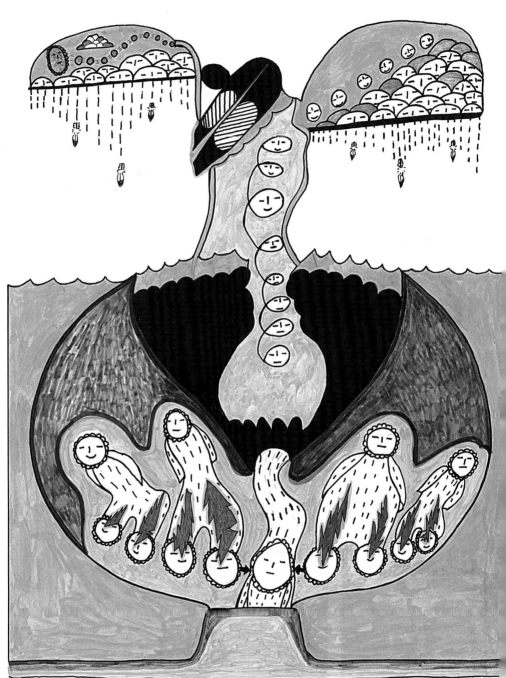

Oceanus vents beneath the Earthly crust, circles of epiphanies for the two Leggeds on Mother Earth in July

A child was conceived in this womb space and nurtured over the years. Now it is grown. I was given this child and this fire ceremony. When the fire is kindled during the fire ceremony in the peace chamber, the light hits the wall and it comes back. Rebirth. Maybe the light that comes out of the walls energizes the planet metaphysically, bouncing off the walls of cosmic consciousness. Consciousness expands as the light touches it and now more is knowable.

For twenty-one years I took care of that child given to me in vision because that was my responsibility.

American Indian religion has to do with developing the visionary capacities of the whole world tribe and of the individual people in it. We acquire these visionary capacities through dance, singing, chanting, and ceremonies, and by keeping that visionary status in the community and following the advice of the tribal visionary. The visionary would get visions for the tribe to enhance the life of the tribe as a whole. The various ceremonies or dances tribes have are based on actual visions that people had. In time, the people who had the visions died, but the other people kept these ceremonies going.

Oceanus
vents
beneath the
Earthy crust,
circles of
epiphanies
for the two
Leggeds on
Mother Earth
in July

sound
and
the
breath
of
god

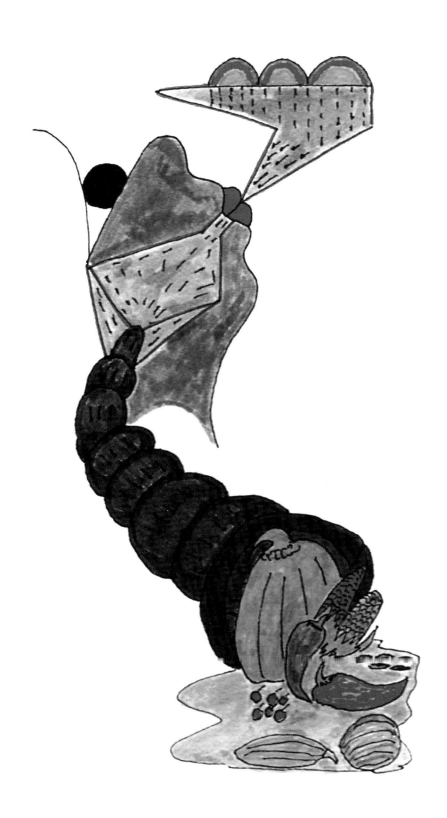

the vision of the horn of plenty

The latest step in my work for world peace has been to announce the appearance of a new vibration in the cosmos. This vibration is the Horn of Plenty.

On April 16, 2006, I was doing a dance in Australia when the Horn of Plenty appeared above the dance ground. The fruits of the Horn of Plenty began to fall into the dance arbor, and the shape of the arbor changed from a circle into the spiral pattern of the galaxy that we live in. From this I knew that this was a galactic vision.

The spiral is the energy or action of germination. We call this *huh-leh-neh*. *Huh* means seed that now is being spread all over. I saw the Horn of Plenty spilling seeds into *huh-leh,* which means they are going to germinate. They are going to germinate on Planet Earth as well as in this galaxy.

In my vision there were all different kinds of seeds. There were some blue seeds, red seeds, orange seeds, yellow seeds.... All kinds of seeds were spilling out, like little stars.

A blue star was the first star to fall from the open side of the Horn of Plenty. It was a five-pointed star, symbolizing five personal gifts to "the people" on planet Earth. "The people" means all life on Mother Earth. The blue star came spiraling in toward the center of the galaxy, bringing new energies and it is changing everything on our planet. As it spirals back out from the center, new forms take shape.

Ah-huh-lah means light is germinating. *Lah* is the sound of the word *light* and in Tiwa means Divine Presence, God Presence. (This is how I think—in symbols.) The Horn of Plenty to me is like a medicine bag. The medicine bag is where the medicine man puts all his powers. Now it is open and it is spilling out its fruits into the galaxy.

Bag is *moh-neh.*

Moh means "to see."

Neh means "the Vast Self and personal self as it places itself in a statement of awareness."

Horn of
Plenty ~
2006

That is the meaning of the bag itself. It doesn't say what the contents are; it doesn't need to. By its very nature the medicine bag holds everything in it. It is self-explanatory what is going to be in there, because it is in that medicine bag which, in this vision, is a Horn of Plenty.

It is spilling out into a spiral, which means it is germinating whatever is being seeded there. And, since the Mother Earth is in that spiral too, the Earth is going to be planted with all those seeds. Abundance is coming to all of us who are living on the Earth at this time and our children, grandchildren, and great-grandchildren.

This vision makes perfect sense to me, because it came to me in 2006, which was the twenty-fourth year after the coming of the sound peace chamber vision. It came to complete what has been started with the sound peace chambers. We were taught in the tradition of my father's people at Picuris Pueblo that when mankind can't do something, then celestial energy comes and celestial vibration takes over whatever needs to be done. What the vision means is that there has been a major shift here. From the germination of the seeds will come the flowering of change. We humans have fooled around long enough, and God is going to take over. From now on, we are going to get plenty of everything we focus on and act on. If we focus on conflict, we will get more conflict. However, if we focus on peace we will get plenty of peace. As soon as we focus on a goal, the universe will take us in that direction.

I want to announce to people all over the world that this Horn of Plenty vibration is here for all peoples of all races of all nations. Now, prosperity and abundance are here for all of us. They are going to show up in many different ways; just pay attention and you will sense, you will hear, you will feel the vibration of a worldwide shift toward peace.

I am an artist and, after I had this vision, I realized that my art was beginning to change, was being endowed with greater and greater levels of the vibration of peace for the whole world.

All of you who read these words will have more and more

peace in your lives. It is important for the future generations that when we elders leave this world, we leave it a better place for our children, our grandchildren, our great-grandchildren. You are here on Earth at this time because you are supposed to be here as their fathers and mothers, grandparents, aunts and uncles. You will pass this peace on to future generations and your responsibility will become their responsibility. Yet, this responsibility for the vibration will be *no* responsibility, because they will *be* the peace of the whole world.

The Horn of Plenty is here now and it is here to stay. We can begin to recognize ourselves as the true peacemakers because we are alive and we are living in this time as the peoples of the global societies.

Summer nights with Mother Earth and her children

song of the living spirit

he storytellers of Picuris Pueblo take the children out under the night sky and point up to the stars. "This," they say, is "*Nah ku tah* (the cosmos). Yet we, the people came from beyond the stars, beyond *nah ku tah*, from the place where life never ends and also never begins — a place of forever."

The cosmos is *nah ku tah,* and *na ku tah key* is the spiral galaxy in which Planet Earth sits. We, the people, came from beyond *na ku tah* (the cosmos), from beyond the stars, and landed to become the land of Planet Earth (Mother Earth) in a place called *nah ku tah key.*

We are the land dancing. We live a life of prayer, of reverence for the land. We live a life of ceremony so that we may stay alive and connected to God. God is present in the land: the soil, the sky, the clouds, the seasons, the climate.

And we are part of that design.

In Picarus Pueblo, stories do not begin with "once upon a time." They begin with with "*chu ha men ten*"— a long time ago. Literally, *chu ha men ten* means "at the sand place." The Picuris storytellers use this expression to mean "a long time ago" because every grain of sand is an eternity and there are many of them.

In sound language, "a long time ago" also can be, "Beauty of being aware at a time light is descending from the up-above, where there were rays of pure clarity" — or — "Crystallizing of no-form into form that the Vast Self might see reflections of divine moments."

Sound language always has multiple meanings because there are so many realities, and it (sound), I believe, does not always know what reality it will become at any given moment. Life, after all, is vast.

What does sand come from? From *naa meh nay*. Soil. Sand is the soil along the ocean, which is a portrayal of the cosmic

Summer nights with Mother Earth and her children

mind. All rivers flow down to Sand Lake. The rivers and seas speak to us of a return to Source, a return to the no-thing. When someone in my family dies and we lay him out, we place a feather on his breast. Just before burial, we remove the feather so that afterwards, we can lay the feather in the river and watch the current bear it downstream, back to the sand place, back to Source.

Ceremonies, metaphors, parables, puns and stories are the teaching tools of the spiritual teacher in every tradition, including mine. Metaphors connect the world around us with the metaphysical, giving us a window on the infinite.

A metaphor is not simply a figure of speech. Metaphor is how God is present in our lives. We think in godly ways because metaphor is energy that is in a state of action, breathing life into ceremony. We work with metaphor in order to find the essence of everything we encounter in the material world, in perceptual reality. We trace it back through metaphor, and when we trace it back, we find that everything is connected to the heavens. When we trace the language, it all ties back to the One.

Everything that exists is trying to unify itself with that whole. All ceremony exists to unify, to bring together, to bring into oneness — but within that oneness is the diversity of all that is.

The ancient storytellers asked us children to go in search of our relatives who stayed behind in that place of forever, beyond *nah ku tah* (the cosmos). They told us that would be our life's destiny, to find our relatives in that place of forever.

The number one in the language of sound vibration is eternal life, that place of forever, where life never ends and also never begins. The oneness is, actually, the only thing that exists. It is the only reality. And it is nothing. Yet from that nothing comes all that is.

The land is who we are. The land is our first significant energy, which we begin to recognize as ourselves. The land is where our power really lies and that is where expanded consciousness can be cultivated.

We know land is Divine Presence because the word land begins with the letter "L." This letter, sounded "el," carries the vibration of a very ancient name for the Divine in many languages. "El," "Elohim," "Allah," and many more names for God carry the "L" sound. Since we too, the people, are land, that would make us people of the Divine.

Indeed, there is a power that every human being has, that cannot be cultivated by reading and writing. We must do something with our physical bodies and natural elements of the land, the fire, water, air, minerals, and wood. Native American ceremonies, some of which are very ancient, and many of the secret societies that Indians have, are based on this intention: to reconnect, over and over and over, to the land. When we keep connected with the land, that is how we can keep our power.

We find life empty and unsatisfying because we do not involve ourselves in ceremony. It is encoded in our physical make-up, by virtue of the fact that we have eyes and ears and mouths and noses and legs, that we are here to be catalysts and to connect the physical with the spiritual. Ceremony is how we do that.

Actually, in a sense, everything we do is ceremony, whether we mean it that way or not. But ceremony is so much more powerful if we do it intentionally. Ceremonies we do intentionally focus our energies on certain acts and lift us into states of expanded consciousness through which we are literally drinking light. We are drinking inspiration from all the heavens and connecting the above realms with the physical plane. This is what we come into physical form to do, and we are nurtured by doing it. If we don't have enough ceremony in our lives, pretty soon we feel empty, sad and dispirited.

We may think we are sad because our physical needs aren't met or we need more success, but what we are really feeling is the natural hunger of the self for connection with the Vast Self. And that can only come through ceremony.

Ceremonies are most powerful if we do them regularly as a part of a community of people who gather for that purpose. They can be done alone; in fact, we came into this physical form to express an individual, particular vibration or essence. But really, we are connected with each other and with the Vast Self, and we need to reconnect regularly, because that is the source of our joy, the source of our energy, the source of our enthusiasm or zest for life.

The ceremonies have to do with chanting. Chanting has to do with sound. Sound has to do with the vibration of the spirit that is in the land. In ceremony, we are the land chanting, we are the land dancing.

There is a voice that is coming from the land. It wants to tell its story, and this is its time. Now the time has come for the land to tell its story.

Morning
Prayer for
☞
➡ a new
dawn

song
of the
living
spirit

Morning Prayer for
→ a new dawn

Spirits of Red Rock

language of the land

One night when I was six and had just moved to Picuris Pueblo, my Tiwa-speaking grandmother said to me, "Chi-pii-you (Go to sleep)," and tucked me into bed. A few minutes later I opened the door to the bedroom and told my grandmother that I could not sleep.

She tucked me back in my bed and in a very soft voice said to me, "Listen to the sound of your breath and you will hear 'Chi-pii-you,' who also is your guardian angel, who will help you sleep." I began listening to my breath, and this is what I discovered: In the inhalation of my breath, I heard the sound "chi" and in the exhalation I heard the sound "pii-you." I felt loved, cared for and secure. Soon I fell asleep.

When I became twelve years old, I had an insight that the Tiwa language spoken around me was a collection of powers manifesting as sound vibrations. When I asked the seven different elders, who were women, my teachers, about how the language happened, they said, "It was given to us by the spirits of the land and sky."

The Ute language was appropriate for the geography of the Ute reservation in southern Colorado where I lived until age 6. When I was taken to live with my father's people in Northern New Mexico, I was taught Tiwa, because it was the power of language for that place — for the Picuris Pueblo. The Tiwa language is an energy that resonates in that geography. I was eating from that resonance, sleeping it, so I needed to speak it. Tiwa was the vibration of that geography, which extended for twenty or thirty miles.

Everything that exists on the surface of the land is really an extension of the land. Ceremonies are about these extensions of land, or how land expresses itself in its highest natural form. And land is the Vast Self in a state of purification. Land is flowing with waters that purify, with rivers, with rain, with snow,

Spirits of
Red Rock

with the ocean like a big lung, constantly freshening the air.

In Tiwa, land is *naa meh nay*. The first sound is *Nah*. *Nah* means Self, the Self in a state of purification. *Meh* means movement. How is movement occurring on the land? How is the land producing movement? How is the land producing placement and connection? How is land connecting the sky and the Earth? As two-leggeds, when we walk our feet sink into the crust of the Earth with each step, so that the Earth and the sky are always walking, and we come along for the ride.

Life is unfolding from the inner recesses of land, which is really the Self, the Vast Self. The land is telling the story. It is not a story about Tiwa people; it is not a story about any tribe. This is the story of the land, the Vast Self, speaking about what it knows it is. This is what consciousness is. Consciousness is the result of how the Vast Self is in a state of movement, how it is purifying itself, how it is placing itself, how it is manifesting. When we look out into the dark sky at night and allow our eyes to drink the millions of lights, we begin to understand Infinite Vastness of Self. Drinking light through our eyes is an activity of our souls.

We have developed a technology around materialism, and after many years of developing the technology, we have come to think that this is a material universe. Yet there is another universe that exists alongside it, and it is called breath. We haven't really dealt with that universe. We haven't understood that metaphor. We have separated ourselves, saying, "This is scientific; that isn't." What we need to do now is understand how the soul purifies itself so that it connects concreteness with abstractness — concreteness, which is the material, with spirituality, inspiration.

Inspiration occurs and in the process it purifies that form of placement that we can now experience between ourselves as material beings and a philosophy or abstractness. We can now use our inspirations to materialize our goals and objectives that are not in detriment to our highest spirit.

When traditional Native American people look at material reality, we are looking not for scientific truth, but for the

CLEAN
AIR
Sacred
holy
Offering
for the
People of
Mother
Earth

language
of
the
land

56

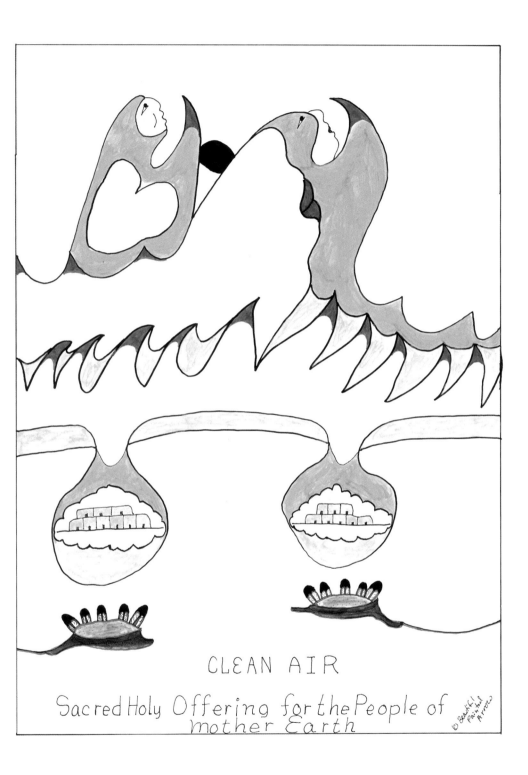

CLEAN AIR

Sacred Holy Offering for the People of
Mother Earth

metaphors. To look at a thing as metaphor is to ask, "What principal idea is it expressing?"

We are born into the realm of discovery. This is the gift that allows us to enter into the world of sound, which is encoded in our gene pool. Another way of saying this is we innately know how to speak in metaphor because the void is the timelessness of what we know as the "here and now." The void is essentially the No-mind. Consequently, as soon as the thinking mind enters into the void of the No-mind, the action of that motion awakens the remembering of the gene pool. It is at this point that we know what we did not *think* we knew.

Everything is metaphor. Everything that exists — every object, every action, every experience — is expressing some principal idea. Therefore, it is important for us, early in life, to pursue ways of conceptualization that enhance metaphor alongside experience. Ceremonies of the living spirit are such pathways. They give us routes to follow so we can penetrate the surface of manifested reality and experience directly the power of principal ideas.

Everything is encoded in the gene pool. Whatever language we speak, we are speaking from that particular culture, but beneath that there is a code that is understood universally. One of the ways to tap into this code is to listen to how we pronounce words. Sounds are important. For instance, the sound "waa" in English is part of the word "one." *Waa* in Tiwa means life. Behind both of these is a common essential idea that is encoded in the human gene pool.

In order to become conscious of principle ideas, we have ceremony. When we dance a bear dance on the reservation or when we dance a corn dance, it is our way of expressing devotion for the Holiest of All Holies. For me, dancing is like going to church. My whole body is in prayer when I am dancing. Sometimes I dance my anxieties, to pray about them by dancing them. When something comes up for me or I need answers, I just go dance. To dance is to expand. We dance to expand our awareness.

When we dance in ceremony, we are expanding whatever

principle we are dancing at that time. For instance, if we are doing the circle dance, we are casting new seeds of understanding, since the seed and the circle are metaphors of the same principal idea. Yet we are not consciously aware of that in that moment, as we dance.

The planet made it possible for us to be here. The planet, the spiritual essence of the Vast Self, which is made up of valleys and rivers and mountains and oceans, is really the concrete formulation of infinite nothingness. Infinite nothingness has now become concreteness, in the form of oceans, valleys, rivers, water, and oxygen.

We need to look at the fact that in our consciousness we have somehow separated ourselves from ourselves and from God. Perhaps we wanted to be better than God. In doing so, we have created disease, because, being separate from God, we have been functioning only at half power.

When we are born we leave the wholeness of the mother. We break off, become individualized. We say, "I'm going to read and write. I'm going to be a master of my own life. I'm going to run my life the way I want to. I'm going to be on my own." That is fine, and we have developed a technology that allows that, but we have separated ourselves more from ourselves, from the Infinite Self, from the Vast Self, from the God Self.

Yet we are really part of *naa-meh-nay*. If you want to know what is wrong with you, go back to what is wrong in the land. The Indians say, "Don't cut up Mother Earth." With all our technology, we lose touch with the land, with *naa-meh-nay*, and when we lose touch with the land, we lose touch with ourselves and with the Vast Self.

The word *naa-meh-nay* tells us that the self is in a state of movement, and movement is manifestation. *Naa* is the self. *Meh* is movement. *Naa meh nay*, then, means that the Earth is the self in a state of movement. The word speaks of closeness to higher planes of knowledge. It speaks of sky energy, of what is up above, in touch with high spiritual beings of all ages.

Land is the principal form that sets up a stepladder to

Planet
Earth

The moon arrives near the Earth to seed abundance in the Oceans

climb to the heavens, because the land is the Vast Self, which is descending light that purifies; it is the purifying force that brings heaven and Earth together and crystallizes it so that it looks like a tree or an elephant or an ocean. Any time you have movement there is manifestation, and manifestation brings perception. When I touch or feel or see something with my physical senses, that is perception.

Matter is in a state of incompleteness; it must have the perception of the perceiver to exist. Matter is temporary. It only keeps its form for as long as we think it is what we think it is, and then we change it to something else. Its meaning is temporary.

I can see thoughts manifesting as if they were lights. I see thoughts travel across a room in little blocks of light about half an inch long and a quarter of an inch wide. There are spaces in between when one of those little blocks of light ends and before the next one begins. These spaces are when that thought is open and is ready to manifest new form, even as it is going along. That is how quickly change can occur. Even as we are thinking something out, as it is traveling twenty feet across a room, it can change.

Life is a circle and the circle means seed. Any time we have a thought, we have just seeded an idea into the vastness, which is made of the land, which is made of earth and sky. The breath is *haah*. *Haah* is identity; breath is identity. Breath gives identity to movement; it gives identity to relationships and to the hierarchy of knowledge as we seek to understand the mystery. Breath connects us with higher levels. Breath is inspiration. Breath inspires things to occur, because the breath is an integral part of how the miraculous is unfolding on the material level, in the material plane. Without breath, nothing occurs.

Breath is what materializes form and gives it a name. Consequently, we as humans are participating in naming many new ideas, new universes, new eternities every time we breathe in and out. The beauty of our lives is that we are already there, living in newly named places, while we are walking along in our lives on Mother Earth.

The moon arrives near the Earth to seed abundance in the Oceans

language
of
the
land

51

We think breath is just physical, but the reason we are breathing all the time is that this is how we stay spiritual. Breathing is how landscape stays spiritual. The land breathes and it rains and the wind blows. One inspiration comes and soon another one comes, and soon after, another comes. In this reality, this land of *wah mah chi* (breath, matter, and movement), there has to be continual inspiration because everything is impermanent. In this plane of reality, there is always a continuum of becoming something we want to become without ever really becoming what we want to become, because that which exists as a state of impermanence does not really exist.

This material plane is where we go to find out how to get where we want to go, only to learn we've already arrived. But we are still trying to get there. The exciting thing is that we are still talking about process. That is what the Earth is about: process. When we understand what process is, then we know why we need to be here.

There is no evil in the universe. Evil in our perceptual reality comes from conscious states of separation in the psyche. The One separates itself from itself and is split into two incomplete selves. In order to be holy, it must be whole.

By participating in the process of a ceremony, we can re-connect ourselves with the Vast Self. And so we dance a circle dance, and we become the power of completion or oneness.

Or, we cover ourselves with clay in a ceremony, and by doing so we remake ourselves back into land. By doing that we reconnect our psyche back from split-ness to wholeness. When we connect to Vast Self, whatever we create after that is going to be inspired by things that are in tune with the highest potential of the planet as a whole.

*We call the claying ceremony an Initiation into Womanhood.
We dig a hole and then someone stands there, and a woman
who is an elder, at least fifty-five years old, puts mud on the
person standing in the hole. As she is doing this, the rest of us
stand outside the hole and we sing sounds. When the vibration
of our voices touches the skin of the initiate and the water, he or
she is initiated into womanhood. We do the same thing for both
men and women. The men initiate themselves into womanhood
so they can unfold in the feminine. We do this so we can now
bring the feminine and the masculine together. Womanhood
allows the seed within life to germinate into the soil of life, the
soil of landscape.*

*We all want to be initiated into womanhood because it is the
feminine that helps us to slip through the crack between two
slices of light, and for a split of a split second, we exist. It is the
feminine, not the masculine, that is that power of inspiration.
When the inspiration unfolds, then it is masculine. The
feminine is the descending light itself, and the masculine is the
unfolding of the feminine.*

*When we initiate women or men, we are initiating them for the
planet and for the cosmos. Apparently this initiation is needed
right now or we wouldn't be talking about it. All we need is a
handful of people to be initiated. Perhaps we could initiate seven
thousand women and seven thousand men over a period of time,
and that would restabilize the planet. Our initiation restabilizes
the unfolding of the feminine for everyone.*

*In ceremony we are rededicating ourselves to the original goal
of the Vast Self, which is the land. The land may look like
Scotland, or Italy, or Germany, or South America or the United
States. But it is really just the Self — the Vast Self.*

Dance Chief calling the Sun-Moon People
from the Spirit World to come and Dance

© 2005 Joseph Beautiful Painter

sound, light, song and ceremony

While sun dancing I had a vision of how God created all that is. I saw a light appear and then it radiated out in an instant, at the speed of light. The sun dance pole, made from a tree, was that point of light, that center from which the circle of light flashed out. When it flashed out, it connected with the mental, emotional, spiritual and physical parts of my being. We humans have four parts. We are emotional, we are mental, we are physical and we are spiritual. And those are the same four parts that make up the medicine wheel.

josephrael.org/
expand.mp3

The flash went out from the One and then it came back into the One and disappeared. In that time, that instant, I knew a lot of information. All that information came as that point of light flashed outward. I saw that as a circle of light. There was no circle until the light went outward from that center point. As it expanded it created the circle. And then the periphery disappeared and the light came back in.

When the light went out, it was being pushed out by space. And when it was coming back, time was pulling it back to the center. In another split of a split of a split of a second it would go back out again in the same process.

That is how life is occurring.

Dance Chief calling the Sun-Moon People from the Spirit World to come and Dance

We dance in order to expand the potential for something to happen. It works because the word for dance is *pu-leh*, and that vibration contains the powers we need.

Pu is the principle energy of "to hook" or "to expand."

Leh is the principle energy of the power to name all creation.

Leh is also the beltline, the area of the navel. In my tradition, when the newborn baby's umbilical cord dries and breaks off, we take it to an anthill and leave it there so the ants take it back into the land. Land is *nah meh neh*

When we dance we usually wear a feather. Feather is *kee-wah*. *Kee* means everything that exists. *Wah* means life. So feather, *kee-wah*, is the prayer for everything to be given life. Now it begins to move.

When we dance for three days, we are dancing that circle and the pole, the center. That is what we take home. It is the movement of the heart, taking life in and sending it out again. Pulsing. It is the movement of the lungs, breathing in and breathing out. It is the simplest, most basic movement of life, a continuation of the Big Bang. Even before then, it was occurring.

When a sun dancer dances back and forth to that pole in the center of the circle Friday, Saturday and Sunday, we can see how much growth the dancer experiences if we measure the space-time — the amount of space the dancer uses over the span of those 72 hours.

To know what space is, I go back to sound; I listen to the sound of the word for space in Tiwa. When I listen to the sound, I learn that space means "to focus." Time is giving us capacity to crystallize ideas of awareness, manifest them, and place them, while space is pushing us, and saying to us, "Come on. Focus! Focus on what time is trying to tell you." Time is trying to tell us to manifest. Time is trying to tell us to place these particular ideas, or awarenesses, as it is pulling us forward. Space is pushing us, and time is pulling us.

Because we are focusing on this particular part of consciousness, it avails itself. It avails itself in many different ways. It keeps repeating itself over and over and over until we get it. We are not consciously aware that it is there, trying to tell us something.

We are dancing to the center pole and back out, to the center pole and back out. Soon we start making a trail or a track. Eventually we incorporate that into our psyche, and we take it home for the next 365 days or so. The Universal Consciousness plugs into our wheel of light, or our medicine wheel, to our mental capacities, emotional capacities, physical capacities, and spiritual capacities. Then, the universe is feeding us. But, like a wind-up clock running down, it runs out after about nine or ten months. It dries up, and so we have to dance again. Dancing, we renew that connection, that pipeline to the Universal Mind that, then, is feeding us the next gifts and ideas we are to receive, the inspirations, the epiphanies.

Space is what is curving time. And that is what is creating gravity — that dialog between time and space. When we dance we expand the light over and over through time. When people leave the dance, they may think they are still in same place, but actually, they've grown from where they were when they started out because of the effort they've made over time.

Whatever we send from the center, such as love and forgiveness, we send them into the past and the future; they curve back in and return to the center.

Chanting helps us to be fully present; therefore it allows us to be in the future and in the past simultaneously. The capacity of time and space dialog gives us that ability. That is why we have bi-location (which is the ability to be two places at the same time.)

josephrael.org/
effort.mp3

josephrael.org/
dances.mp3

You have to move, because movement also gives you the capacity of perception. You get an idea, but you're not going to be able to understand the concept without movement. Remember that this universe operates on the basis that somebody has to be looking at what is going on. The universe has to step back to "see" itself. The universe has to send out its voice to hear its echo. Perception requires movement.

Our physical bodies are principle ideas. As we move our physical bodies, we bring all those principle ideas back into the center, back into the Universal Consciousness.

What happens when we dance ≈ As we move for 365 days, then the grid turns into a wheel; it comes back at a higher vibration. It comes back because of gravity. It turns into a ball, a sphere. The outside of planet Earth is that sphere.

We dance the dance, and the vibrations, or patterns, or powers are awakened by our dancing, and all those principle ideas we are expanding as we dance go out over the surface of the Earth along that sphere, and they can be felt for the next 365 days in various places around the world. Certain things are going to happen on the Earth because of the principle ideas we have danced. And because we have ten fingers, we have ten potential possibilities to manifest something. There may be five or ten different discoveries or inventions that come about because of that dance.

Dancing and hitting the sundance pole so exhausts your regular energy patterns that the mind, which is holding the pattern of the ego self, just finally lets go. Then, you can see beyond the self to the larger pattern. You see that you don't exist, that you are a part of a bigger pattern, the pattern of all life. Life is movement in cycles, like our galaxy, which is a spiral in motion. With each cycle, we climb higher and higher toward heavenly spaces.

After sundancing, I had a vision in which I saw in a circle of light going out and coming back in to the center in an instant. As it came back in, it brought me knowledge of all that was and was to come. I saw a map, and I saw Indians as islands being swallowed up by European-American culture. They were still holding the American Indian vibration, but they were being swallowed by the technological European-American culture.

American Indian children were sent to Indian schools to break their vibration and remake it in the pattern of the English-speaking world. Remember that any language is the vibration of the people who speak it. Indians were forced to break away from speaking the language of the land and to speak English, the language of technology. Today, as the children of technology, we no longer have access to the realignment that used to happen naturally as a result of our speaking the language of the land. We have a different mindset.

The mind creates ego energy systems that have to be broken down in order to realign. In order to get back to that original vibration of God's love, we have to realign to love over and over every day. Ceremonies can realign us, but ceremonies become rote over time. Everything becomes its opposite, and when ceremonies of the Living Spirit become rote, they lose their power to realign us. We have to keep finding ways to be tuned once more to the original vibration of God's love.

When we dance we are expanding the energies, those vibrations for which the dance is intended. During the long dance, which is done at night, we dance and dance and dance, and then at some point, maybe three o'clock in the morning, we'll have an epiphany and we'll suddenly see how the energy is all around us, moving very, very fast. And we will have a picture of it. That used to happen to me every time, so that is how I know that the energy is going all around the Earth.

I created three dances — the long dance, the sun-moon dances, and the drum dance, for these spiritual gifts.

The drum is the sound that can see the inner essence of the soul. The drum will help you to reconnect your life to your soul. You hear the beating of the drum and the vibration that comes out of that has the power to take you into the inner recesses of yourself.

During the long dance, when you are dancing in the darkness, you are dancing in the night light. The night light, or dark light, is the power to call forth, let come to you, that which you are searching for. You're calling it for yourself, but you're calling it for the whole Earth and for the planets and all the other galaxies of the cosmos.

Every dance, every ceremony, is both for you and for the cosmos.

And even when I sit down to breakfast, that, too, is a ceremony. Any time a human being acts or moves, that movement is also a service to the cosmos, because of who we are.

We dance because we humans don't move out of this reality until everyone is ready, and our dancing helps for everyone to get ready, to consciously evolve through the spiritual ceremonies. I'm stuck here with you and you're stuck here with me because somebody over there is lagging behind. We have to dance in ceremony to try and help him along. We don't have to tell him anything. We are going to usher in a new day for him while he is watching football on television with his remote control.

josephrael.org/
music.mp3

josephrael.org/
origins.mp3

Song
of the
baskets

sound,
light,
song
and
ceremony

60

Song ≈ There was a moment when Song began. At that time, beauty, heaven and pure clarity glued themselves together and fused themselves to that moment to become Original Chant. In the next instantaneity, the sound crystallized and now it knew that it could be, and that it was a possibility. Heaven, beauty and pure clarity disappeared into each other, and that was a moment. And that first moment was a chant, was a sound, and that made it possible for us to have space-time, and all that came with light and gravity—all that is.

And so, everything that came out of that original song is music. All there is is music. You have your vibration and I have my vibration, everybody has a particular vibration, and so we are all singing our personal songs. From the time we are born as babies, when we are middle-aged, when we are old, we are singing our songs. Because we are vibrations, we are the holy ones, we are the sacred ones.

What is song? It is light. And what is light? It is wisdom. And what wisdom is doing here, through our bodies and through these walls and this room and these roads that we build and the cars and everything, is just a big orchestra playing together in harmony. That is why we sing … to remember that we came from song.

Chanting helps us to be present in the future and past simultaneously. We can use song to access the past and the future because all events, future and past, are all going on at the same time. We are all always in the future and the past, even when we don't think we are. Even when we don't have the intent to be. Because that is the nature of the chant that we are. It is just that, in *this* dimension, we are taking it in increments of time. We are here for thirty minutes … half an hour. In this dimension we slowed it down so we could see it, so we could remember it, and so we can enjoy it. That is what we are doing here. Here we get a chance to perceive Universal Intelligence that looks like somebody advertising their business on a billboard, or somebody waving a white handkerchief because they want to hitch a ride home.

As soon as someone starts to sing, he creates the Infinite Vastness. The Infinite Vastness encompasses billions and

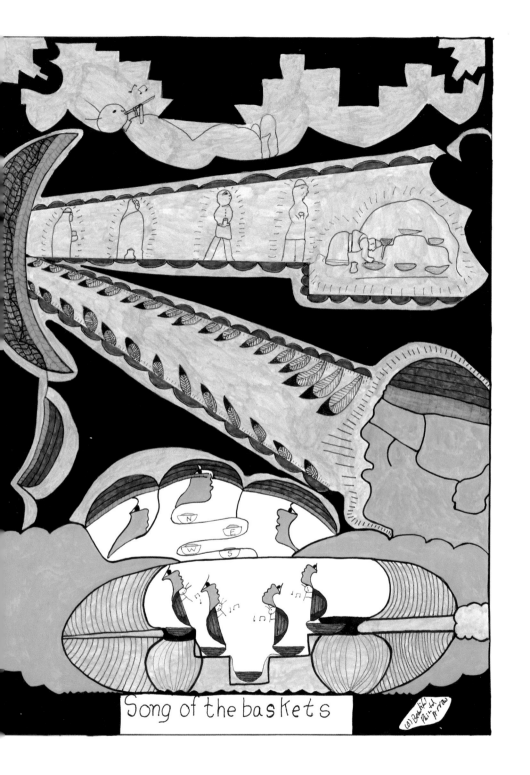

Song of the baskets

billions of light years. He creates that in that song and fills it with innocence. Now we are teachable, now we can learn, now we are being blessed. And that chant also gives us the power to carry — to carry ourselves as two-leggeds, the trees to carry themselves as trees, the oceans, the mountains, and all of the eternities. It is in that "cha." It is in the resonating, flowing, vibrational essence. It is in the Great Being of celestial light. And that celestial light is the work that is done by pipe-carriers.

Bi-locating ≈ I have had the experience of bi-locating, of being in two places at the same time. When that happens, I can pick where my consciousness is located. One second I can be in one place and next second I can be in another place … consciously. I don't really like bi-locating, because I think that is boring. When you bi-locate, you're not really experiencing either place. You are seeing one reality through an overlay of the other, so you have two experiences going on at once. When I see something, I like to see it very clearly, very distinctly and precisely, and so I can be here, okay, and then I can be over there, fine. When I'm here, I just want to be here and when I'm there I want to be there. Then I can see each of them in turn, clearly.

When I think about it more, I say, "What was that about? Why was I attracted to that moment, that I would want to experience it in that way?" And I never get a satisfactory answer for myself. The answer I get, I'm not always happy with. But I guess I don't have to be happy with it, because later on I find out why it has happened.

I cannot pick when I'm going to be able to bi-locate. I think that is possible, but here is the problem with the idea of being able to bi-locate intentionally. The element of surprise is gone, and I think there is something about the element of surprise, the unexpected, that is really a very important principle. If we set goals that say this is what we are going to do and we don't have the facility of the unexpected, pretty soon everything would go just the way we wanted it, therefore under our control. As soon as we have everything under our control, life is not dynamic any more. At the end of time, we would look back and say, "Maybe that wasn't the best choice I made," because by then we may have more knowledge about what the potentials might have been.

How much security do we really have on this planet? All Mother Earth is is just a big rock going around the Sun, so let's enjoy the ride!

The other part of it is that we don't exist. We are being what we are seeing.

Parallel Realities ≈ We are walking on two planes at once. When we are walking on a plane, there are two vibrations that are walking, one to the left of us and one to the right of us. The two vibrations are always only one, even if one vibration is in the ordinary reality and the other is in a parallel reality. Consciousness is actually a tricky dimension because of its many pathways going on all the time.

While in this dimension, millions or billions of years may go by; in other dimensions that I know of, those eons are like slices of light. We have the power to extend those slices of light into millions of years in perceptual reality, but we are also functioning in other realities that we don't perceive here because they fall between the slices of light.

We have the ability to live with total joy and appreciation because we've finally made it to this level. We are two-leggeds now, and each moment is a time of appreciation for life.

We don't exist because we are creating our realities as we are going along. Because we live in a collective consciousness, everyone is contributing to that creation of our shared reality. Yet, we are dying because we are not drinking light. We have created self-imposed limitations. We created them because that would help us create knowledge that would help us achieve the things we wanted to achieve materially. We have done that already and so we are now at the next phase, but we are not going to go to the next phase until everybody gets on the train.

You are the song. You are the sacred. You are who you are and it is good.

Beautiful Painted Arrow ≈ The name Beautiful Painted Arrow was given to me by my Picuris Pueblo grandfather when I was a child. This is a traditional name in Picuris, and it is the name of a particular arrow – a medicine arrow.

In tradition there is an arrow that the hunter carries with him that he never uses, but it is a sacred arrow – a magic arrow.

If you are carrying one of these arrows and you get lost, you pray on the arrow, tell it what to tell the medicine man, and you shoot it. It goes to the medicine man and talks to him.

Song Stick ≈ All the songs of our people are in a piece of wood.

They're written on the stick because the stick talks to the medicine people and teaches them the songs.

Everything has a vibration. Everything is energy. Everything is alive.

Vibration is made of the power to crystallize an idea. An idea can be very unclear, and vibration can bring in all of the intricacies, all of the different levels of resonance, so that now the idea has potential to crystallize. That is how we have understanding; cognizance. Vibration can fuse the idea with awareness. Vibration has the power to crystallize something from nothing.

Vibration is going on all around us and in us. Most vibration is not audible. You can't hear it, but it is there all the time.

Vibration also has the power of placement. It has the power to crystallize an idea, fuse it with awareness, then place it in the hierarchy of up and down. Once you've done that, once you have crystallized it, you have the idea in its full capacity, its full empowerment.

Plants are doing this all the time, but as two-leggeds we are at the cross between the vertical and horizontal, are at the intersection of the mental, emotional, physical and spiritual. We exist in that vibratory presence.

Beautiful
Painted
Arrow
song
before
Painting

sound,
light,
song
and
ceremony

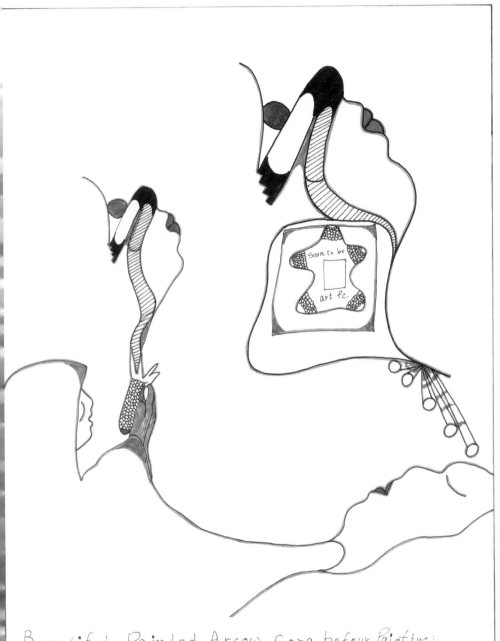

Beautiful Painted Arrow Song befour Painting:
    'Oh Grandmother help us to see."

(C) 2008
Beautiful
Painted
Arrow

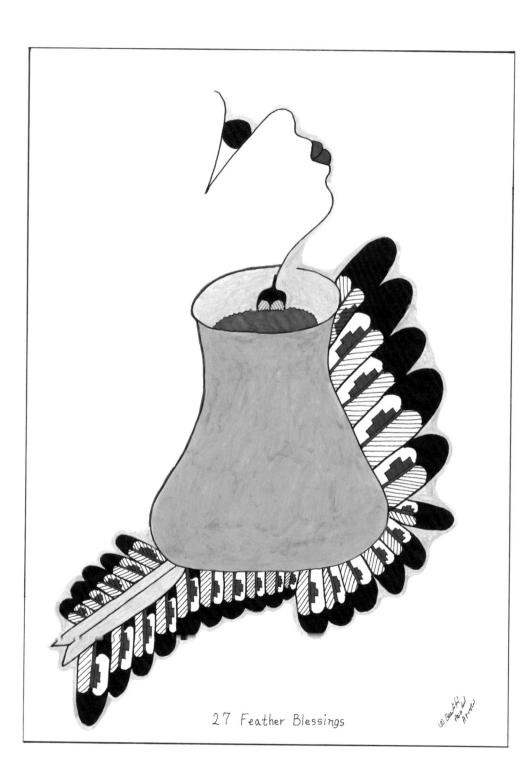

27 Feather Blessings

Eagle feathers and spiritual light ≈ Remember images are forms that come out of the dark light of potential and take form in material reality. As above, so below. Look for metaphors. Look for synchronicities; every synchronicity has meaning. Learn to think like that and you awaken capabilities in the brain, so that soon you're giving people readings of the hidden meanings of things.

Everything is vibration, and vibration is light, and light is Universal Intelligence.

We venerate eagles and we dance with feathers because eagles fly very high in the sky, near the sun. There are two kinds of light that come off of the sun. One is physical light and the other is spiritual light – the power in your brain and physical body that allows you to become inspired.

The eagle feather carries that vibration of spiritual light.

We take the feather and put it in the water (basically hydrogen and oxygen, the most abundant elements in the whole universe). We leave the eagle feather in the water for two or three seconds and it fills with spiritual light. I bless you with light by splashing the water on you with the feather.

You don't have to believe it, I don't have to believe it, God doesn't have to believe it. I just know it works. It works every single time. You've been blessed with light, which is universal intelligence, and now that you've been blessed with the eagle feather, you're going to want to learn things.

You can learn by paying attention to what is around you. Every animal — the dog, the bear, the fox, the coyote, the armadillo — they all represent certain celestial powers. You can track that armadillo to a principle that you can study. You can study a fox every day of the year for fifteen or twenty minutes and, even if you live to be 110, you wouldn't know all the mystery that is involved in just the fox. Every single being is an opening, a door, for you to learn the greater mysteries.

I think the last place that we are going to go as a human race is where the American Indians have been. The Indians have been studying these different animals for thousands

sound,
light,
song
and
ceremony

of years. Our concern is that many of these animals are disappearing. They mean a lot more than just animals. They are gateways to other levels of intelligence that we haven't honored, we haven't captured yet.

The physical body is a composition of many, many principle ideas. Take, for instance, the face. The eye is *che*, which means cooking. The Mother/Father being who created eye-ness is Beauty. All Beauty wants to do is be teachable. The nose gives you the power to expand on whatever inspiration you have received. Anything that comes out of inspiration is going to be successful. Always. Or, look at your feet. Feet have to do with awareness. The baby learning to walk is aware of its surroundings. It holds on to the wall, the chair. Every time you walk your foot energy goes down into the ground. Every time we walk we are activating awareness. It is programmed into our bodies. Awareness is always with us.

Soul is the same vibration we get when we drink a glass of water. Every time we drink we are affirming that we have a soul. Fasting is *peh-pi-oh,* which means to give death to that we think truth is. As soon as we give death to that which we think truth is, then the real truth comes in. Otherwise we are limiting ourselves, and we never get to the real, basic foundation of truth.

In the Picuris of my childhood was the knowledge that each moment we recreate ourselves. Each moment we change. And everything around us, everything we do — breathing, walking, eating, fasting — we are activating awareness of the principle ideas behind it all. Everything in the cosmos comes from an idea. We don't exist. We are creating our own reality as we go along. We are caught in the dimension of space-time. In each moment you are a brand new person and I am a brand new person.

The universe is set up so you can't lose. The universe is open to you; you are not an accident. Think of this as a key moment in your life and try to get as much out of it as you can because you're never again going to be in this moment.

I think God laughs a lot.

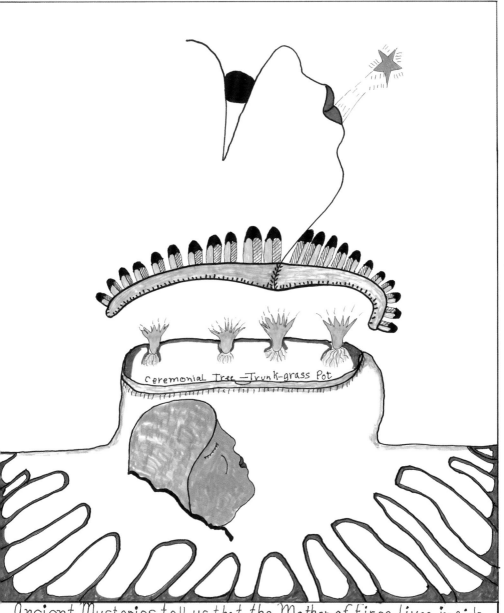

Ceremonial Tree —Trunk-grass Pot

Ancient Mysteries tell us that the Mother of fires lives inside the roots of grass, the roots of trees or in the brightest star in any night sky

taa-meh-neh-father

WINTER
AUTUMN SPRING
SUMMER

Key-aah-neh
mother

The Cosmos dreaming us in and out of perceptual realities

(C) Joseph Beautiful Painted Arrow

creating reality

Consciousness is how Universal Intelligence is manifesting into something that matters. And that something that matters is what creates the principles and the ideas in those principles that make the mystery of life. One of the resonating vibrations of that mystery is that it is creating awareness. Every single moment Universal Intelligence is creating awareness.

In order to understand the mystery of life we have to understand all the different phenomena that are going on around us all of the time, including the seasons and what is happening in spring, summer, autumn, and winter. We have to understand what is going on in the moment and how the moment is important to mystery and how that mystery is unfolding. For instance, the tip of the human finger is a mystery all in itself. We could study it for a whole lifetime and not get the bottom of that mystery.

Each moment is an opportunity for song to express itself in vibration, and the song that is orchestrating in each moment is what is being created in each moment in that Eternal Now. So, in order to understand the mystery, we first have to understand how we are in it — how we are participants in the mystery. By understanding how we participate in the mystery, we can understand that we *are* the mystery.

For instance, a fish swimming in a river is very much in the psyche of every human being, though some live all of their lives and never see a fish. An elephant in Africa is very much part of the psyche of all human beings, though they might live all of their lives and never see an elephant. And each human being is in the psyche of every other human being so that there isn't one of those human beings that is alone. Even though they never meet each other, they're still very much in each other.

We don't exist. The reason I say that we don't exist is that we are creating our own realities as we are going along. So, if

The Cosmos dreaming us in and out of perceptual realities

we are creating our own realities as we are going along, then the only time we exist is when we are creating a reality that we can reflect upon. We create this reality through thought. We create it through how we think life is unfolding. And yet we don't know where we've been, except in recall. We are the creators of all the realities that are going to occur because we are the manifestors of reality.

When something is no longer applicable, it ceases to take form. We are not making many lances anymore, or arrows, because they are not applicable to our culture. They are obsolete; they don't matter anymore. We don't all ride horses anymore because we go out there and get in our Cadillacs and Volvos. That is our new metaphor for the horse.

You see, we don't really need to drive cars. Easily and quickly, within a few hours if we had to, we could come up with other means of transportation—means that don't rely on material things like cars. But we have chosen to drive cars because we are trying to get to Beauty materialistically.

We are not going to get there that way, of course. The way to God is through inspiration. But because we are connected to the economics of our time, we move according to how much money we can make, and so we are trapped by our own desire for economic security and we miss out on creating nonmaterial modes of transportation. There are many inventions that haven't appeared because they are not proper to the social, political, and economic systems we have created. They are not in line with what we consider to be self-preservation.

The true inspirations will not come until there is true poverty. As long as we continue to have plenty of cars and airplanes, we will continue to have that form of transportation. But suppose there is a scarcity of aluminum and steel and rubber tires. I would guess that within twenty four hours we would have an invention. Within a month, we would have a whole other kind of system going for transportation.

In order to understand why we are doing what we are doing today, we have to understand the goals and objectives of people 150 years ago. And, as we change our ideas about reality, we change reality for people who come after us. That is because, when we change our ideas about reality, we change our actions. We go to a different orientation.

Perhaps someone in Albuquerque a long time ago looked up toward Santa Fe and said, "I am going to have to be there in three days and I wish I had more time with those people up in Santa Fe, but I'm going to have to walk maybe a day and a half to get there, and I wish there was a faster way." Well maybe somebody thought that 150 years ago and now we have cars that take us from Albuquerque to Santa Fe in an hour. Somebody thought of it and then later materialized it and now we have pavement and we have cars and we complain because there is pollution in Albuquerque and Santa Fe. But somebody dreamed it up back then. Be careful what you dream about, because you'll probably get it.

Each individual is an individual because God wanted individuation. So each individual will look at something and have a different visual of that something. This is because Creator wanted to look through the eyes of every single human being and be able to see something different though each individual. This way, Creator is not looking through just one single vision, but through the eyes of all.

Each of us is creating our own reality. And yet we think that, because we are one human talking to another human being, we are all looking at the same reality. When we begin to educate each other that everyone is having the same vision, seeing the same reality as us, we begin to encourage sickness, because we are no longer existing in many different realities. We are existing only in one. Then this begins to directly affect the human psyche because we are no longer allowing for new creative intelligence to be continuously existing from moment to moment. Rather, we have decided we wanted to make it so that everyone would see only one reality, rather than six billion realities going on simultaneously.

People try to convince other people that what is important is just one reality and those other realities are not acceptable. When we start to believe we exist, we open ourselves to the mindset that only one reality is "true." Once we do that we lose our understanding that there are really multiple realities. We try to model realty into one, and then we fall into the vibration of judgment. We judge what we think is right and what we think is wrong, and then we are stuck. Once we are stuck, we fall into decadence and that eventually leads to the death of the psyche.

Yet, the universe is trying to lift. There is a light-like band of energy, full of the power of lifting, that encircles material reality as the atmosphere encircles the Earth. This is the part of the Self that is lifting so anything that comes from there is going to kick you upstairs. This force is lifting the Vast Self.

The Earth is made of spirit (winds, thunder, lightening), mind (land), and body (movement within matter). The Earth is made of *wah mah chi*: *Wah* means spirit; *mah* means mind; *chi* means body.

Speaking in very general terms only, an idea is given birth into linear time following these steps: First, the spirit (*wah*) breathes, inspires the idea to become. Secondly, the mind (*mah*) brings it into a place of manifested consciousness. Now the new idea has a mind. Finally, the *chi* is the movement of the new idea in the physical body. Hence, life is breath, matter, and movement.

The movement of the Earth around the sun is the force that pulls the idea from spirit (sky) into the Earth, captures it in the land (*mah*) and gives it movement (*chi*) (eyes to see, as in perceptual reality). An idea is born.

The wind comes to bring to the Earth two parts of carrying power, one part of awareness, one part of Self, and one part of movement. It is what provides us with the Breath of Life. The thinking and the No-mind bring us transcendence as they teach us how to crystallize our completions and how to find awareness in our lives. They teach us how to keep on plowing awareness into our Beauty that is filled with good works. And too, That-Which-Comes celebrates when we find ourselves in the actions of the Infinite Right Action.

Energy
spheres

creating
reality

74

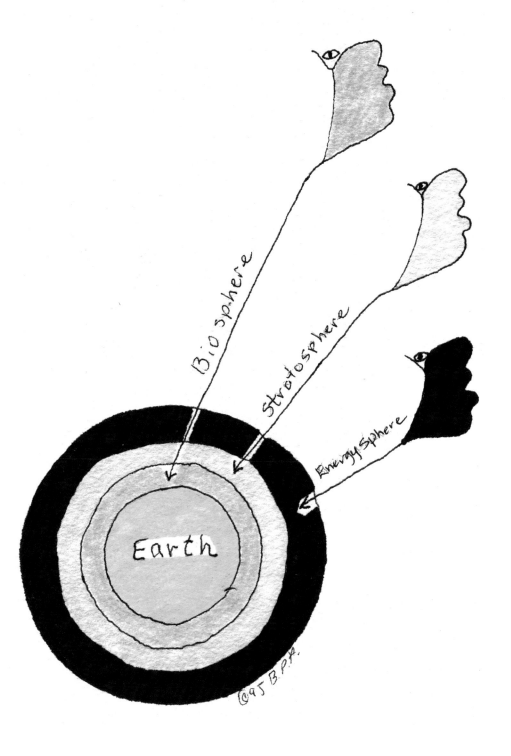

Ceremony for Severe Cyclones with Strong winds

song, dance and the human brain

n the weather patterns of the Earth we have lows and highs (pressure systems). In Tiwa thought, this pushing and pulling, heating and cooling of air, this work, is the same thing as worship. ("Work is worship," my grandfather told me.) In other words, these highs and lows are how the electromagnetism pulls in ideas or pushes them out from the core of the Earth to the biosphere, stratosphere, and the realm of pure ideas; or from the realm of pure ideas to the stratosphere to the biosphere.

These understandings of how new ideas take form in material reality are Tiwa teachings. Of course, the Tiwa elders did not use words like stratosphere and biosphere. They taught in metaphors, and in the Tiwa language, which is itself rich in metaphor.

Inside the human brain is the thalamus — the relay or association center which integrates emotions with experience. The thalamus is at the "heart" or center of the brain, and it lies beneath the cerebrum, the seat of rationality, which is at the periphery of the brain. In Tiwa thought, the center, or heart, is connected with hot, with summer, and with emotions, while the periphery is the place of the cold, rational winter energy. In the pueblo, we have summer people and winter people whose activities in this Earth plane balance the hot with the cold through ceremonies.

Ceremonies awaken the child's memory. They are done once a year so that we re-instill a pattern in everybody; we awaken that ancient process by which the heart and the mind create balance in the living Earth.

The dances Indians do awaken ideas toward expanding holistically, because during the dancing the body heats up and cools off, thereby integrating the mental and emotional bodies.

As a child I was taught that two-leggeds — humans — came to this Earth to bring reconciliation. Our job is to be the

Ceremony
for
severe
cyclones
with
strong
winds

catalysts for the reconciliation of ideas. It is a part of the process that began when the unity of the Vast Self began to perceive itself as diversity. Out of that diversity came polarity. We are here to act on that polarity to help bring about reconciliation.

We are the catalysts for this reconciliation because we have two legs. In the process of walking, we balance and reconcile polarities of left and right. The word for "walk" in Tiwa is *tah chi who*. *Tah* means to plow, or to seed; *chi* means movement, especially a movement of reconciliation; *who* means carrying, or right action. Inherent in the word *tah chi who* is the understanding that by walking we are implanting this Earth plane with the sort of movement that will carry, or bring balance — that will reconcile polarities. As we walk our destiny as two-leggeds, we will find ourselves designing new technologies that are in balance with our ecosystem. This is our specific task as humans. We walk so that we can transform ourselves — genetically and in other ways — to continue our evolution.

Henceforth, new technologies created by mankind will be more in tune with the needs of the Earth and sky.

All ceremony originally came from a vision somebody had which gave instructions for exercising mystical power. The instructions were passed down from generation to generation unchanged, because if they were changed they would lose their power. The Tiwa creation stories were told over and over, from year to year, using exactly the same words. They still are. They are only to be told in the winter. They aren't just children's stories; they are really a source of mystical power. The storytellers repeat the stories not just because the new children coming up need to hear them. The very pronunciation of the words of the stories affects the psyche of the planetary resonance. It is affecting not only the Tiwa speaking people, but all of the world, from New York to France to the polar regions. That is why it is very important to tell these stories in the same way every time.

The same thing is true of any traditional ceremony that belongs to a people or a tribe. It has to be done in the same

josephrael.org/
reconcile.mp3

Woman
of the
Mounain
Lakes
calling

song,
dance
and the
human
brain

Woman of the Mountain Lakes calling for Mountain Rains— in Ceremony for the Water moon

way each time to work, whether it is a ceremony for healing or for bringing rain or for whatever purpose. The Picuris stories are sacred and their telling is a ceremony. They were never to be written down in their exact form, and one man who told them to anthropologists to be written down was banished from Picuris for life. When I was studying art in Santa Fe Indian School there was a lot of discussion among the Puebloans that we shouldn't be selling pottery or weavings or paintings if they had the Pueblo's sacred symbols on them, because a person can't sell sacred things.

For these reasons, I don't teach Picuris (Tiwa) religion or Ute religion. I teach what has come to me from my visions. I spent fifty years becoming a visionary so that what I do in ceremony comes from Source and it works. I don't know how these ceremonies work or why they work, but they work. People who criticize me for sharing ceremonies with non-Indians don't understand that the ceremonies I am doing are not traditional or tribal.

I believe that ceremonies provide a way of bringing people who really want to know the Spirit into the context of the Spirit, so that they will know their own inner source and how to bring that forth in their lives in an active way and awaken their own spiritual awareness. Maybe that is our job, to make that connection with books or art or ceremonies. Maybe we help that awakening to manifest in a quicker way for individuals who want to pursue the mystical resonances of their own inner sources into blossoming forms. To me, that is why we write books and create art and music.

Now if there were 500 people and I said to them that I am a visionary and everything that I do comes from my vision, 467 of them might say, "We are not going to be involved with it because you are not coming out of scripture, and therefore we are not going to believe that." If they want to say that, that is fine. Remember, we live in *perceptual* reality. Perceptual reality has five aspects, and one of those five is purity. Purists say, "If it is not real, then I don't want it." Yet I believe we are all visionaries and that we come out of inspiration. After all, we have been breathing since we were born, haven't we?

We get an idea, we get inspired and decide that this is how we have to do it now. We say, "*Ah-ha!*"

"*Ah-ha!*" is the word for inspiration; it is also the word for breath.

The ceremonies I describe here are not done in the way I describe as Tiwa traditions or a Southern Ute traditions. I am here to create tradition. Everything that I do, I do from my visions. The ideas that we are getting come from the heavens — from that band of light-like energy that is full of the power of lifting.

The planet knows what it needs. Often we don't understand the message and we go off in left field. I believe this is because we still think we are better than God. We have to get back to our integration with the land, and then our thoughts are going to be in tune with environmental consciousness. That is my job. That is what I chose to do when I finally ended up with two feet and here in this lifetime. Consciousness was just unfolding in life's greatness and having a great ball of fun. Soon enough, I was more than a twinkle in my father's eye and I came and I was born. Now here I am, and I am part of an ancient people who believe that the land is the Infinite Self and that what it means to be a human being is to have vision. We honor the visionaries in our world as seers because of what they know. They have given their lives to do what they do, and they are the only ones who have accessed this information until some time when everybody will have access to it.

A visionary knows the meaning behind very ordinary things. For instance, what does it mean when you are walking down some stairs and there is a low ceiling and you accidentally hit your head? In a metaphor, it means that the universe is asking you to focus on something. You notice that when you hit your head.

Maybe you feel stupid. I think that what the psyche is saying is that there is separation between thought and body. Thought and body need to be put together again. To me the body (including the feelings) represents the land, the Vast Self.

The thought and the brain are what come out of the Vast Self, but then the brain sits up there on its throne and wants to run things, control things. That is fine for a while, but eventually it has to understand that it is not independent and it has to merge and come together in the vastness of the Vast Self in order to touch reality.

Technological society encourages the separation of the mind from the body. Our educational system and everything that we really value in Western culture separates us from Infinite Self.

I have heard certain speakers say that clergy took our spirituality and doctors took our physical bodies and the universities took our minds, so we are a separated, fragmented society. We rely on specialization, whereas in the beginning everything was all one being, one thing together. We are fragmented in the house of shattering light—which is consciousness. What we want to do is get back together again.

Unification has to be done almost all the time, and that is why we have rituals and ceremonies we repeat. Every several days we do a ceremony to reunite again. This is the power of the ceremonial cycle. The effect of each individual ritual accumulates over time as it is repeated. By having a monthly ceremony or a weekly ceremony, we reinforce our connection to the whole, like the nerve connected to the whole brain.

The Catholic mass is a good example. In Catholicism as I see it, as soon as you go into that setting, into that church, you go back into the Infinite Self, back into the soul, back into the center, back into that part of you that you separated from. It is like returning to the womb. There are symbols that the genetic pool knows and the unconscious responds to. A candle is the light, the truth. The priest is the metaphor for the inner self, that is, for the soul.

The drink is the sweetness of life, the wine, the sweet blood of life. It is in the cardiovascular system on the physical level, but we are not talking about physical so much as we are talking about the spiritual cardiovascular system, the mental cardiovascular system, and the emotional cardiovascular system.

The bread is beautiful light. When two or more come

together and break the bread they are eating beautiful light. As they do this, they remember on some level that they are the light of beauty.

The being of emotion is breathing, it is thinking. It is perception. Perception has to do with knowing — knowing through the senses and also knowing beyond the senses.

I think someone has already said these things. What we are doing is making it so ordinary and natural that people are really going to understand it. Because it *is* natural, and it is all around us, and it is made of land and movement and breathing.

Land is *naa-meh-nay*, which is the Self fusing itself with matter in a way that has a relationship to everything else that is happening at that moment in time, and connecting to all the heavenly planes. *Naa-meh-nay* exists so that the Self can connect to physical materialism and to the spiritual aspect of Earth.

In Tiwa the word *naa-meh-nay* is what the land is doing, what land is being. When we say *naa-meh-nay* it is not a fixed thing. *Naa* is Self, *meh* is movement. Naa-*meh-nay* is the Self that purifies, that connects the material to the spiritual through movement.

To the degree that we lift ourselves to a higher level of being we have physical movement on the planet. And we keep lifting. When we have Earthquakes and disasters, we suffer loss. Perhaps people die. Yet, we can look at it both ways: we can ask what is the lesson? What is the blessing? If I am a materialist, I will say, "No! It is not good, because I just lost five parking lots in the Earthquake. That was my income." Maybe the gift for me in losing five parking lots is that now I'm going to have to figure a different way to make a living. And in the process of figuring that out, I am going to change my psyche and that is going to give me *naa-meh-nay*, the Self in the state of movement, manifesting something new.

Naa-meh-nay is telling its story. If we will listen carefully, perhaps we might reconnect ourselves for an instant to the heavenly planes. Perhaps we might, for a split of a split second, really exist.

Blessing place for school books

the story of creation

n the village of Picuris where I grew up, there is a stone we call "the Blue Stone people," which is a sacred site. Many times during my childhood I saw the elders of Picuris coming to the stone to honor the Blue Stone people and give them corn meal.

I was in my grandmother's house in the early 1940s when I had a vision. I saw a transparent ship come down from the heavens and land next to my grandmother's woodpile. In the ship were two kachinas. They were very tall and they were wearing black and white robes. They got out of the ship and moved north from the west end of the house to where they stopped, and the next thing I saw, the Blue Stone people were there and the kachinas started feeding the blue stones. I just took it for granted that maybe they were using cornmeal to feed the stones.

I was five or six years old when I had this vision. I had just moved with my father and brothers from the Southern Ute reservation to Picuris. I was a new arrival, just there maybe a week. My mother hadn't come to live with us yet and we were living with my grandmother at that time.

Half a century later I had another vision of the kachinas coming. In that vision, I was in the sky. There was a hole in the clouds and I could see down through the hole. I could see the top of Picuris Pueblo as if I were looking at the village from the sky.

It was as if there was a book in front of me, a thick book, and as the pages turned, the landscape of Picuris began to change. When the kachinas landed it was a mud flat with nothing there. As time began to move the pages (for each page was a moment in time), I saw the whole landscape change. It was like a wind was blowing the pages over, and many, many pages later, eventually we had a river and vegetation there, and eventually we had the village on the other side of the river. As

Blessing place for school books

85

this all was happening, I realized that the kachinas had turned into vibrations, and that was what was making the pages turn. Those vibrations were creating the vision that was inhabiting that landscape, the place that today is Picuris Pueblo. I still did not see any people there at that moment. Then the vision ended.

It is interesting that the Tiwa creation stories tell of beings from outer space who came here to seed the planet. That is part of the whole concept of consciousness, the concept of the upper world seeding the middle and lower worlds (the lower world being the land, the Earth). These beings seed the Earth with ideas—vibrations that enhance *naa-meh-nay*.

Out of the seeding emerges everything we know, according to the vision I had. The kachinas plant the seeds of what we know now as the circle of life or the sacred circle, or the medicine wheel. They bring time and timelessness. Nothing becomes something. What happens is that they seed the Earth, which is the vastness of the Vast Self. They come from above; they come down on a transparent ship; and then they go back into the heavens and translate what this all means psychologically; and then they come back and land, not really landing on land. They stop descending, and things take material form. Infinite Vastness is the beginning. That is what they land on. According to the vision that I saw, this is how spirit descends into matter.

Another way to say this is that in a split of a split second, a flash, a principal idea descends from the realm of pure ideas into the Infinite Vastness. This realm of light-like energy is full of lifting potential, so any time inspiration comes, it is because a thought has gone up and imprinted itself there.

From this realm comes a downward flow of energy, undifferentiated energy, feminine energy, spirit. Infinite Vastness stops the downward flow of this spirit energy. Spirit falls until the Infinite Self stops it. It is still perceptual, not material. It is impermanence. Then it lands on the floor of life—the Infinite Self.

The spirit is different from the Infinite Self. It is transparent.

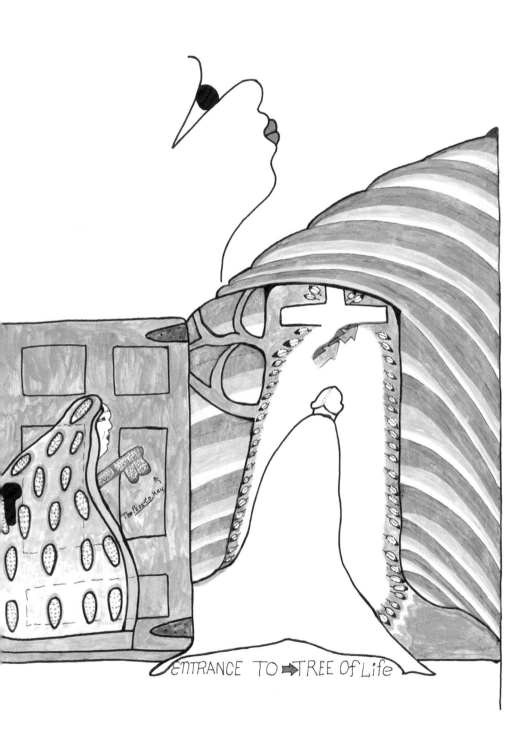

ENTRANCE TO ➡ TREE Of Life

It is like nothingness coming down, and it merges with the Infinite Self and becomes something.

Another way to say this is to consider the Tiwa word *waa*. *Waa* is light descending–*waa*, as in the English word, *one*. One is everything coming together; one is up above and down below, north, south, east, and west. *Waa* is the light that precedes creation.

It meets the Infinite Self and it is then two. Two means to *cry*; two means we can say, "*Hello there!*" or we can call out, or cry in tears, because we are now in reflection, in duality. We can now mirror, and we are the image.

The Vast Oneness has to split into the Vast or Infinite Self and spirit before anything can happen. As in the process of biology, the cells separate to make more cells and make life.

After separation, spirit and the Infinite Self come together in a different way. The way in which they come together depends upon inspiration, which is the breath, or the imprint of the movement of *nii*. Inspiration is materialization in which placement or relativity is an enactment of motion, and which instills wisdom in the act of making this placement in this moment.

At first water covered everything. Then, after the waters started to recede, the land was there and it was just a lot of rocks. Then the winter came; I could see the snow, and then I could see it melting and then it was summer and it was hot. I could see the cold and the hot and the cold and the hot — winters and summers and winters and summers breaking down the rocks until they were sand. Finally there was a tree growing there. I saw it grow to be an adult, and then, finally, it fell. In Tiwa the tree is called *tslah-ah-nay*, which means greatness. When it fell, I realized that that is how the land was imbued with greatness. This first tree awakened the memory of greatness, because it is the essence of greatness. When it hit the ground, and as it started to rot, it gave us time. The rings in the trunk of the tree tell us that time expands out from a single point. It doesn't expand inwardly—not in this dimension, anyhow. Time begins with a seed of light, but once it goes out, it doesn't go back to the point of light until it breaks up into soil as humus. Then it goes back into the One, into the beginning. You can look at a stump or a cross-section of a tree and see how an insight might happen, beginning with a seed or a single flash of light and traveling out from there.

The ancient traditionalists used to use trees for ceremony. In the ceremonies they would dance around a tree or climb a tree or hang things in it, or dance back and forth as we do in the sun dance. The tree is a symbol of how time is expanding and how we are expanding as a part of that greatness or expansion. It is the symbol of the movement and expansion of divine thought or divine essence. The tree is the most concrete substance that we can see and touch that connects us to how greatness is expanding.

So, after the seeding takes place, then there is *existence*—All-that-is. The most elementary forms of life appear, the fungus appears, then other plants and other forms of life. I saw this unfolding very rapidly in my vision.

Also in my vision I saw the mountain form, and the flow of the water from the mountain to our village, to Picuris. The mountain is the heart center, because water flows from the mountaintop in streams and rivers, like the arteries coming away from the heart.

I saw the rivers going to Picuris, then I saw a place southwest of the center of the village. There was a crack and I was taken there, and then I was looking at it, and then, in the next instant, people appeared.

First, there was nothing, then the Earth cracked open and a gas-like substance came out, and there appeared a group of people, maybe sixteen of them, standing there. They were already there, but now I saw them. They were Indian people, Native American people with bows and arrows like the grandfathers. Three or four were elders, and there were young men and women, and then children eight or nine years old and maybe a baby or two.

According to my vision, the kachinas came down from the northeast, then they landed at the blue stone. Then, the Earth

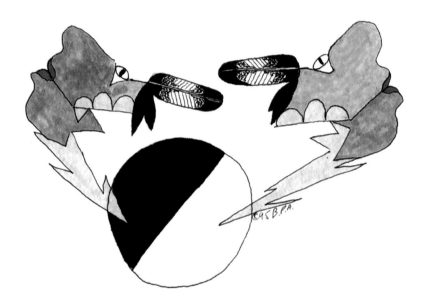

The Winter Summer People

formed and the waters receded and the mountains rose up, all very rapidly in my vision, though it must have taken millennia in reality. In the next instant, a crack appeared to the southwest of the center of the village, and the cloud appeared out of the crack. And when it cleared, the people were standing there.

I think it is important that they appeared in the southwest, for in Native American thought, the direction of the southwest is another gateway or sacred transition point. It is the same as that instant in which summer becomes fall.

There is a continuum that is the line that goes from northeast to southwest on the medicine wheel. This line, or axis, divides all-that-is into the male and female.

Along this axis, the people are separated into the winter people and the summer people. This line separates the autumn and winter on one half and the spring and summer on the other.

On this axis, in the northeast is where the black and white kachina beings landed. The northeast is the place where winter becomes spring. The winter is when things are in the womb, and spring is when they are born as idea, so the northeast is the time of seeding. Then, the idea that is seeded goes around the wheel through spring and into the summer and to that point where summer becomes autumn. That is when it is born as material reality. That is when the energy has "cooked" and what was seeded as idea takes material form.

The winter is the place of inspiration—states of inspiration. But what is interesting is that inspiration occurs not in that space which is to the north, or in the wintertime. That is not when inspiration happens. It happens right when winter ceases to exist. There is an instant when inspiration stops and spring occurs. On the intersection of two slices of light—at that line—it happens. A new idea enters, moves sun-wise through springtime into summertime and then, when it passes midsummer into autumn, it physically appears. This appearance happens at the instant when summer becomes fall, or in the southwest. Here it "falls" into material reality. Then it matures when it gets to true west. Then it goes to the north

The
Winter
Summer
People

story
of
creation

91

where it is infused with spirit, with the fullness of inspiration, moving sun-wise around the medicine wheel.

In my vision, the beings landed from outer space right on that slice of light between winter and spring, and thus between the spiritual and the mental realms, at that place where they intersect. That intersection is the beginning of the idea. The inspiration is formed above, then it "springs" forth as idea.

Remember that at the beginning of physical manifestation, there was a crack on the Earth. This is because the kachinas, or beings from outer space, came bringing power, energy. They *became* this energy and they permeated the whole planet. They landed in the northeast, and in the southwest is where they materialized. They materialized out of nothing. In the material realm I saw them land in the northeast and they became an energy that was about three feet off the ground and they looked black and white like kachinas. Black-and-white represents mental energy. (White is the house of the shattering light, and black is breath, blowing breath.) They were at first mental forms, and then in the southwest they became people who in my eyes looked like native people.

Before they were native people, however, when they were here as kachinas, they landed in a transparent ship and the next thing I knew, the land was going through a transfiguration. This transfiguration is important because when an idea descends into consciousness, it comes down and it goes into the Infinite Self and it materializes and goes through a transfiguration. All the patterns are now changed. Something new has been added.

Then, maybe five billion years passed as the Earth was forming. It took that long for it to occur in linear time, in material time. In timelessness it was a split second. Then the people just appeared out of the core of the Earth

In this way, the original idea became physical; that is how powerful it was. At that instant I saw that the kachinas had seeded the whole Earth.

Millennia had passed and people appeared. "People" means vibration in metaphor. The language that was spoken at

From the
Clay of
Life "the
people"
became
visible

story
of
creation

92

Summer | Winter
People | People

creation
Clay Pot

From the Clay of Life "the people" became visible

© Beatien Primo Morrow

Picuris, then, was already seeded in the ground, so that when we ate from a garden on Picuris land we were actually eating the energy that would identify our culture, identify our speech or our worldview, based on what we were eating from the land that had been seeded with energy. The energy looked like soil, or it had fused itself to become soil. But soil is also the Infinite Self—*naa-meh-nay*—the Self in a state of movement, creating a greater clarity of the relationship between the physical and spiritual realms.

We people are constantly in a state of creativity; we are co-creating.

Creation requires splitting. An individual cell creates by splitting itself. The cell occurs first in the northeast, and then it travels. Maybe it takes a fraction of a second or maybe it takes a day, or two days or five days. Then it splits when it gets to the southeast, and now you have two separate cells.

It is right in the biological makeup of the consciousness of matter: In order to reproduce, life had to split itself. In order to become ourselves, we split ourselves from our memory of ourselves.

That is the reason we have to keep rivers pure and clean, because rivers are our direct way of remembering how to reconnect ourselves to the heart. They flow from the mountaintop, which is the heart center. Today we go skiing and go to the top of the mountain to reconnect ourselves to the heart. Moses went to the top of the mountain and he brought down the law of what is right, of what is connected to the heart.

At the heart center, we know that we are not really split. We appear to be split, but our split exists only in the material realm where perception rules our reality. But this reality is constantly changing, for perception is impermanence.

Ceremonies, like the dances we do, are to help us perceive in this impermanent, perceptual, material realm the reality of the spiritual. People respond to the ancient ceremonies because these realities are in our memory banks.

All visions are always present. A vision is what the visionary is seeing, and what the visionary is seeing is something that now the Being is choosing to perceive. When we see visions, they enter perceptual reality. In perceptual reality, the visionary is seeing something in front of him or her that is now available to be perceived by a perceiver, who has allowed himself now to perceive.

A vision is the soul drinking light. It starts with descending light, like falling rain. The descending light is the feminine, the receptive. It is just light or undifferentiated energy. To someone perceiving the vision, it looks like a picture, or a phenomenon, but it is really just the action of the soul drinking light. The visionary transformation happens in the act of perception. The soul, or consciousness, or the Vast Self is drinking light that looks like awareness. It looks like receptivity; it has the quality of "as-above-so-below." It has the quality of "heaven is here now." What you want to achieve is here now, ready, given. Earth is fused with it; therefore, we can materialize it now and make it real.

That light is innocence. Everything is now open to learning; everything is now open to curiosity. Now we have the potential of creating from it what it can be or wants to be. Now we are given the energy. The vision gives the perceiver the energy—physical energy as well as mental, emotional, and spiritual energy. "Do it!"

Above all, the vision connects the personal self to the Vast Self. In fact, it is all simply the Vast Self *seeing*, making something perceptual because it is going to materialize it. Without materializing, the land can't exist—the land, which is a metaphor of the Vast Self.

You see, the Vast Self is total nothingness. Nothing. The Earth is simply a concretized, slowed-down energetic being that ended up material. What the Vastness sees is what it creates. But, because it is creating what it is seeing, that vast seeing that it is doing is creating a lot of interrelationships— interconnectedness and relationship connections. Perception does that by its very nature. Perception is a connector, a linker. Everything is linked to everything else. Hence the storytellers tell of Spider Woman weaving the web of life. All these ideas tie into the reality that there is a Seer seeing everything. We call it God, the higher power, or whatever. It is simply the Vast Self seeing itself creating itself.

In my mind, however, I see a transparent ship come down with two beings; and they have white and black stripes, and these two kachinas are wizards. This vibration, then, seeds the land and the sky.

This power that lands from the up above, which appears as two beings in my vision, has several attributes. One is the ability to fall—"topple-ability." It is able to topple and to fall. The attributes of falling came from the heavens, not from the Earth.

It also gives us the freezing capacity, to freeze everything in place. We can conceptualize now, can harden. But we don't want to stop the energy at the level of the cold, rational idea. It needs to move through us or we ourselves get locked into that crystallization in the intellect. We act from fear and we become resistant to new ideas. One of the primary struggles in human consciousness is the resistance to change. We tend to get stuck in the forms. We get an idea and then five minutes later we want to keep it alive forever. We need to let go so a new idea can come in.

I tell my students that if they are stuck, if they are resistant to new ideas or change, there is a meditation they can do to get rid of that resistance. Bring some light down through the top of the brain, then through the heart, and then on down through the bottoms of the feet, into the Earth. What this does is connect the upper, middle, and lower brain with inner self, and with the Vast Self. Then, bring the light energy back up through the feet, through the heart, through the brain, and back out to connect to all the heavenly planes.

An idea comes in totally cold, freezing, from the up-above world. It has to go through heart to ground to infinite vastness in the Earth, then back up through the heart. When the energy goes back through the heart the second time, it now has heart energy—feeling, emotion. It goes to the top of the brain, then it is ready. We can now present the idea in a more balanced way.

It is when we do not connect ideas to the infinite vastness and the heart in this way that we have wars. We are stuck in cold reason and we act from self-righteousness and fear. But we can act from love when we use meditation and ceremony to bring that cold intellectual energy down through the heart center, connect it with the Vast Self, and then bring it back through the heart to the brain.

We make that connection with meditation and ceremony.

Ceremony is to awaken our memory of how we are connected with the Earth or the Vast Self. Many of our ceremonies are done on a seasonal basis, once a year, so that we re-instill in everybody that knowledge, reawaken that ancient process by which the heart and the mind create balance on this material plane.

The planet is made in the same perspective as the human brain because we are a product of the Earth, of the geography in which we live. In terms of the brain, the top, or cerebrum of the brain is winter. The lower, inner part, or thalamus, is the summer. The energy has to descend from the top of the brain to the inner part of the brain. It has to fall, to connect with the heart and the Vast Self. When it falls, and then returns again through the heart and brain, then we have creation.

The top is the mind and the bottom is the heart of the brain. The top is winter and the bottom, or heart of the brain is the summer.

Thus we have the summer/winter dialogue. At my pueblo, all the people are divided into summer people and winter people. If your mother is a summer person, then you are a summer person. If your mother is a winter person, then you are a winter person. Summer people live down at the heart of the village, while winter people have their homes up around the village on the hillsides.

At my pueblo, you always belong to your mother's clan,

rather than to your father's clan. If your mother came from the Water Clan and your father came from the Eagle Clan, then you belong to the Water Clan and the *little* Eagle Clan, but you always belong more to your mother's side than you do to your father's side. I think it is because the descending feminine energy precedes the existence of the male.

Thus, if your mother was a winter person, you would be a winter person, too. You would be part of the vibration of the *chi*, or the intellect. If you were a summer person, you would have the vibration of *maa*, or the heart. At Picuris, we do ceremonies to balance those energies.

In modern technological society we are unbalanced, with too much *chi* energy. We think with the head or intellect, and then articulate with the heart. But the intellect is judgmental. When we act from the intellect, we act from a base of fear. What we need to do now is to think with the heart and articulate with the head. The heart just wants to love, so that when we are directed from the heart, we act from a base of love.

In order to clear our brains of judgment, we should stand on our heads. We should reverse our usual way of thinking. Instead of sending ideas directly out from the rational brain, we would move the energy into the Earth, and receive vibrations directly into the brain from the Earth, which is the vastness of the Vast Self. The brain would send them up through the heart, up the legs to the clouds and sky, to be articulated in purity.

The rational mind says that whatever it cannot understand is not real, and that misconception is what separates us from God. Thus, when we create in a technological society, we get in trouble, because the brain thinks, "I am better than God. I am better than the natural world." It thinks that the only things it can bring into existence are those things it understands; whatever doesn't have meaning to the rational brain is not appropriate. That is okay, because that is how we find out we have to give it up, to let go and let God.

Eventually, we have to go back to God. We have to go back to our faith, to our religion, to our belief, and back to ourselves. I am not saying that we need to start a religion or anything;

From the
hand of
the Great
Spirit
comes all
Blessings

story
of
creation

98

'From the hand of Great Spirit comes all Blessings'

© 2006 Joseph Beautiful Painted Arrow

it just means that we have to go back to love, back to the Vast Self, and then we are truly creating from that space of devotion, of worship.

The only time we can *not* be in love is in this body. This is because we are God's echo, but our struggles to exist in perceptual reality can distort the sound we reflect back. God is love, but when we get out of tune with that vibration we are like people singing off-key.

Where does evil come from? We are not tuned, so we don't echo God's love.

Each person comes in with his or her vibration, and we do ceremony to realign that vibration with the echo of God.

Remember, we don't exist. We are packets of energy vibrating on and off. We think our life is a solid continuum, but actually we are systems of vibrations, interfacing with other systems.

Ceremony tunes our system. Movement tunes our system. Alignment cannot come from the mind. Therefore, in order to realign, we do things to take the mind out of it, to distract the mind, so the spirit can get in there.

Movement is our work. Work is worship.

Let's not take this out of context and decide, now that we know this, that everything is going to be all right because we have figured it all out. Life is not about figuring things out. It is about realizing that everything is unfolding in a very natural way. Eventually, those principal ideas will manifest in material, perceptual reality, and new things will have become possible on Earth.

Remember, life is movement. It is *nay*. It is manifesting placement, which connects us with the new thing that has now entered. In other words, we move into a relationship with the new thing that is coming into form. We move up a notch.

I think what we are doing in this plane, actually, is that we are remembering how we became perfect through materialization. After all, this material plane is perceptual in nature. In reality, there is no time; everything is happening all at once. Time is only perceptual. We have broken it down in pieces of time so we could perceive it. We are curious and we want to experience it. It is just like being in a story.

In my vision I saw the different eternities in which we operate. I saw it all as a beehive. It looked like a mound, like a cone. Each cell where the honey is stored is an eternity. There are all these bees flying around saying "beeeeee, beeeeee." We are in a state of "bee"ing-ness in this eternity. Each of these cells or circles is a memory that we are recalling right now. But when we finish, we want to go to the next circle, and the next circle. We are going to be in one circle or another forever.

All that memory is, is how the Heart is remembering. We are remembering how the Heart experienced fear to become whole, how the Heart experienced separation to become whole. Because the only way it wanted to do it was through illusion. So the Heart is the great Being, the great Mystery. All that is here now is a reflection of a Being who lies in a state of dreaming and is perceiving, in reflection, what already is.

This *waa*, inspiration, or life energy enters or falls from the realm of light-like energy. In its falling, this *waa* energy is pure female energy, full of potential. The instant it hits the biosphere, the instant it is stopped, it is transformed to male energy.

Now, this energy begins to move around and upward in a spiral. It splits, part of it spiraling sun-wise, or clockwise, and part of it spiraling moon-wise, or counterclockwise. And in these sun-wise and moon-wise spiraling motions, it forms the medicine wheel.

The falling energy enters at the northeast. As it hits the core energy of the biosphere, a new movement is awakened. Until the feminine energy enters, the core energy is lying down, asleep. The feminine awakens it. Now it is a new masculine, spiritual energy, spiraling upward.

Part of the awakened energy becomes intellectual, or *chi* energy, and moves clockwise. It enters in the direction of the northeast and travels to the east as undifferentiated idea. Then it moves to the south, where it becomes emotion and learns its place within all that is. Now it begins to dance its dance or

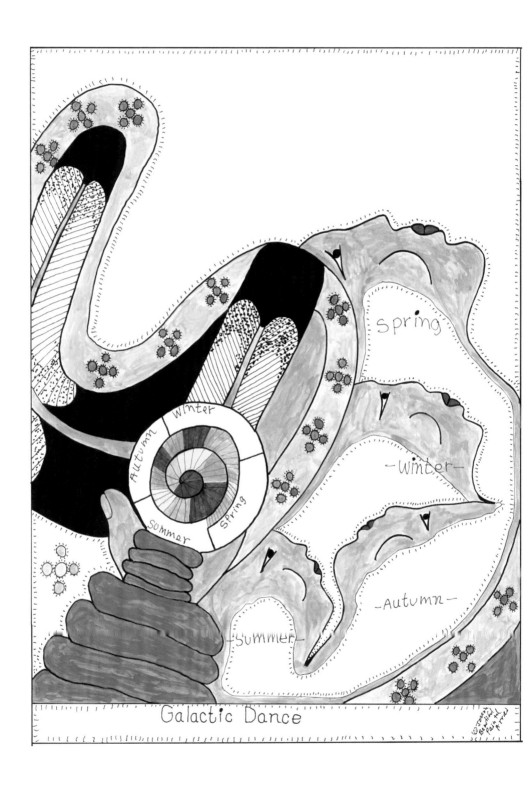

Galactic Dance

sing its song. Then it spirals on to the west, where it becomes physical. The dancing emotional energy takes on pattern and this pattern is physical form. Then it spirals on to the north where it receives a redoubling of spirit and lifts. This is the clockwise movement of the energy, the intellectual, or left-brain movement.

At the same time, part of the energy moves counterclock-wise, or moonwise. This is the spiritual or "*maa*" energy. Entering at the northeast, it spirals to the north, where the energy receives a new infusion of spirit, which lifts it. Then it moves to the west, where it takes on pattern or physical form. Then it moves to the south, takes its place in relation to all that is, and begins to dance as emotion, then it moves to the east where it is purified as idea. The moon-wise movement of energy is the spiritual, right brain movement.

The spiraling energies form a double helix that lifts. Now the All-that-is can express a higher purpose, a fuller awareness. Perhaps that is why the ear of corn is so sacred to native people. Corn provides the image of the double helix in the way the kernels of corn are arranged around the corncob. The Pueblo people believe that first woman and first man came from the corn, from a male/female stalk of corn.

The spiraling energies, sun-wise and moon-wise, form a double helix, lifting. As they lift, the consciousness of the individual is pushed upward. What was formerly not possible becomes possible. A higher level is attained. This higher level now becomes the new ground of consciousness, and the process begins again. More new ideas are received from the feminine life energies that fall from the realm of pure ideas. These energies enter the medicine wheel at the northeast, spiral in the double helix, manifest, materialize, spiritualize and lift consciousness still higher.

This is the movement of the perfection of consciousness.

All ceremony is about this process, this breathing in and spiraling of energies sun-wise and moon-wise. All ceremony is designed to enhance this process and bring about the perfection of consciousness.

Galactic
Dance

story
of
creation

103

water fall of insights

flowering of —
new —insights

inspiration

Life is made of breath, matter, and movement.

One of the qualities of inspiration is awareness. When we are inspired, awareness appears in the psyche of our being. At the moment when inspiration occurs, a new consciousness fuses itself with the personal self. Inspiration is coming from the Infinite Self and it fuses itself with the personal self. This is a physical thing. It happens in the physical body, in the flesh.

Then, heaven comes onto Earth. In that instant, the below and the above come together. Now you have connection to all of the heavens, and there is a flow of energy that wasn't there before.

That energy fuses itself to the heart, to the center of that consciousness. Now loving attention flows. The emotions are involved. Celebration occurs.

Immediately there is awareness again. This second awareness substantiates the original awareness. The original awareness came just to the self, to the mind. Now the heart is involved and the heart and mind are one in awareness.

At that point the inspiration creates a flood of light—a radiance. This is what creates the ecstasy. "Ah! I've been inspired! I have an idea!"

After that "Eureka!" moment of celebration, you have the bonding. In that instant, the inspiration connects itself to everything. It creates a whole. It connects the heavens and the Earth and it creates empowerment.

Once again, in the moment when inspiration appears in the psyche of being, awareness fuses itself with the self, the self fuses itself with the heart, the heart fuses itself with awareness. Awareness creates a radiance, a sense of light, of knowing. It creates linkages and fuses itself to a sense of relativity with everything else. Everything is placed in its proper perspective.

Heaven and Earth come together. There is no longer up above and down below. They become one.

flowering
of new
insights

Inspiration comes with the physical act of breathing. It comes with the inhalation, not the exhalation. Also, I think inspiration is a close relative of oxygen. It is a physical, not a mental phenomenon. If you want inspiration, stop thinking. Thinking will block the process. Instead, forget what you're trying to do and just breathe.

Actually, true inspiration comes when we *aren't* breathing. It comes in that moment between the exhale and the inhale. It comes when we don't exist, when we momentarily disappear from being.

In order for inspiration to bring about creative action, there must be purity, placement, awareness, innocence, and carrying.

Purity is the process by which the heart uses the art of struggle to achieve awareness of its relationship to the Vast Self. Purity then takes that vast infinite awareness and connects it to the personal self. This crystallized thought or personal awareness can now be used as the key to unlock the gate between the physical, knowing world and the spiritual (breath) plane. The breath, or spiritual world, is the world from which inspiration appears. Inspired thought, or an idea, comes as cognizance or understanding to the thinking mind. Now it can be formulated into an impulse for a creative action.

We have the idea of one vast Infinite Self-awareness and the idea of a personal finite awareness, and then we have the process by which these two awarenesses interact.

Think of a circle. Everything outside the circle is the vast infinite awareness that is undefined because it is in the "no-form place," and it is not knowable at this stage to the individual person. Everything inside the circle is that which is already known to the individual and is the current ongoing reality of the person, his beliefs, values, and attitudes. In the

process of interaction new wisdom enters as a mental form from the vast Infinite Self into the circle of the personal self.

Infinite vastness enters the circle, as east energy, as mental impulse. As the mental impulse comes in, it ignites and awakens an emotion. (It moves to the south on the medicine wheel.) Next it expresses itself as a physical impulse (i.e., moves to the west), and finally as an inspiration of spiritual wisdom (north). As it circles, it completes its journey in the inner psyche of the personal self, at which time it formulates itself into an idea to be acted upon.

Through the action of movement in this process, the individual materializes or brings forth into the perceivable world a new clarity of inspired knowing.

The Medicine Wheel ≈ The medicine wheel contains the five principal vibrations or ideas that are in the five vowel sounds:

East = **A** = purification

South = **E** = placement

West = **I** = awareness

North = **O** = childlike innocence

Vertical (up and down) = **U** = carrying

The purpose of *purification* is to clear out all types of pollution. One practice is breathing. In the inhalation, you give life to all the forms being created in you. In exhalation, you clear them back into formlessness. The exhalation—the out-breath—is the pollution cleanser.

In chanting, you will be owning your forms and then discharging them within the rhythm of breathing in and out. You breathe in (own your forms) and breathe out (let them go).

Chanting, then, is a rite of purification. There are many forms of purification rites in various cultures. The traditional sweat lodge is a purification ceremony. Catholics go to confession and receive absolution and Holy Communion. Other Christians have similar purification rites in connection with Holy Communion. Even running is a purification rite, because when we run, we sweat. We run off fat or run off our problems.

Purification ceremonies help us humans to deal with our fears, both imagined and real.

Placement gives us a spot on the planet in which to exist. Placement deals both with location and with what we do and

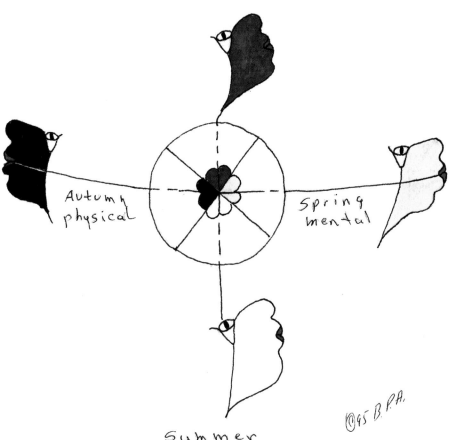

believe. Placement is important, because at a certain level of consciousness, we do not exist.

What is placement's function in our lives on the spiritual path? First, we are on a spiritual path, whether or not we are conscious of this. Everything on planet Earth is alive with breath and is spiritual by its very nature. Placement gives us a way by which to focus ourselves on the life that surrounds us.

We practice placement by focusing on the place on which we stand. When you are ready to deal with a current situation in life, sit or stand still. Stop all physical motion. During that moment of placement, your focus brings clarity.

We may place ourselves in a physical geography, or on a landscape of philosophical leanings.

Placement brings us new potential. In the moment of placement, we are whole, complete with crystallized knowing. Now something is comprehensible to us. Now there is more than enough psychic energy to enjoy the satisfaction of our completed realization, and more than enough energy to carry out the idea.

medicine
wheel

inspiration

The word understanding is a good example of this state because it carries within it the idea of placement. When we understand a concept, we literally stand under it. Our placement connects the creative insight from above with the ground, with our material, physical world.

Creativity is symbolized by a ladder. The ladder represents both creativity and caretaking of the land—the land which is made of the Vast Self.

The vertical line symbolizes realization, the coming into form of the new creation. The new creation is based on unconditional love in a state of inspiration. The horizontal lines symbolize the various levels we are on as we are moving upward toward purity and clarity. We are given a task and resources to help us move upward. One of the resources we are given is the physical body. Our mental, emotional and spiritual bodies are the tasks we achieve through our physical bodies.

Rainbow Makers

We are creating mental, emotional, and spiritual bodies as we go higher and higher towards purity and clarity.

This is the symbol of doing or action, as well as knowing. Our original beliefs or values become the foundation for new awareness. Placement is both at the horizontal line and at the bottom of the vertical line, connected with the Earth.

New awareness annihilates our most recent level of knowledge so that we can become more aware of the next higher level of knowing. We cannot leave our current level of understanding until we let go of it, and we can only do that when the unexpected occurs and we are surprised into new awareness. It is in this process of unexpected knowingness that the old knowledge we were attached to dies. Now the new awareness can come into being.

One of our passionate attachments is to what we currently know. As with jealousy, anger, greed, pride, and the other passions, our attachment to what we know is a mental obscuration that blocks our ability to learn and grow. We are attached to our latest knowing until new knowing arrives.

Innocence means to seek awareness, to surrender completely to infinite vastness and to ask for the self-imposed limitations to be removed so that teachability can happen. Innocence is made up of three vibrations:

The vibration of being in search of awareness or self-knowing.

The vibration of the search process itself.

The vibration of crying for a vision so that beauty may be found.

Carrying is the same as initiation. At sunrise, the sun's light initiates the day. At sundown, the sunlight initiates the night by ending the light of the day and beginning the dark of night. Similarly, life is carrying all that is; all plants, animals, and things. Life initiates us into linear time. We live from one moment to the next one. We live inside each moment, then it passes on so that we can become something new. A past moment that just died carries and becomes the foundation for the new knowing that was just born.

Rainbow Makers

inspiration

111

Our ancient ancestors help us carry our new knowing because they return to us from the infinite vastness that looks like land here on Earth.

Ceremonies of Dance ≈ In the creation myth when we were created as life, we came from the black light into the white light. The black light is light that is in a state of motion, in a state of blowing darkness. Blowing blackness, or blowing breath, is both breath and matter. (Remember that God means breath, matter, and movement.)

We reconnect ourselves with our source by doing a long dance in which we dance in a circle throughout an entire night. For half the night we dance sun-wise (clockwise) and then we turn and for the rest of the night we dance moon-wise (counterclockwise). The long dance is performed at night because the night light is symbolically the "blackness" or black matter, and the long dancer is the symbol of the "blowing" (moving) aspect of blowing darkness.

Again, symbolically, the long dancers are the blowing as they dance in the dark blackness of the nighttime light. Additionally, the long dance is performed at night because the dark spaces between the stars are our origin, our symbol of birth into this life. And as the dancers look into the night sky they know intuitively, through their genetic makeup, that this is true. The black light is how matter and the breath are together in the act of materializing different shades of light (dark to light).

Matter is black light that has been changed into white light so it can be seen as lighted stars or as materialized forms on this planet. The movement part of breath, matter, and movement is the slowing down, the cooling, of the blowing blackness into physical crystallized solids that make up the starry night.

We, as humans, are slowed down (cooled down) energy that has crystallized us into ideas that came from the blowing blackness. We, as humans, will have tendencies to get stuck in the forms that we create because it is in our nature to do so. It is in our nature because we are made of energy that

"Those that fly like blowing wind."

inspiration

Story Tellers Say that
 Ancient ancesters traveled through time looking for
new places to Live and were known as
" Those that fly like blowing wind."

Angels of Light -08

has the potential to be liquid, solid, or gas. We become moon-sun dancers, long dancers or drum dancers to break the crystallization—to free ourselves from our self-imposed limitations.

We were made in the same way the Earth was made by blowing blackness. Consequently, when we dance we do it for the Earth as well as for our personal selves. And this is how we serve the Earth.

josephrael.org/ break.mp3

Today we know, because astronomers tell us, that a supernova made the original elements that make up the Earth and those who inhabit the Earth. The supernova that created our planet came to create our galaxy long before our sun was made. It is told in a Tiwa prayer:

"We came from the night time into the daytime,
And they carry us as
The People."

In dancing we move from our crystallizations that keep us imprisoned. As our bodies move in the dance, we momentarily disappear. Upon our return in the next instant, we arrive with a greater clarity of our senses and feelings. We connect to a resurgence of vitality, physically as well as emotionally. Our inner organs begin to breathe with less and less effort; mental blocks are released. Our psyches can now redefine them and assist in the restructuring of the newly claimed self.

Angels
of
Light

inspiration

As we release mental, emotional, physical, and spiritual blocks, we sense and feel beauty—beauty in ourselves and in all beings in life. We have successfully connected the personal self to the radiance of Divine Beauty. The expansion that has been created allows us next to have new inspirations for new challenges in life, and we begin to see problems in our personal life as opportunities for growth, rather than obstructions.

115

Ceremony and the Essence of Material Forms ≈ One of the first things I learned while at Picuris is that everything is alive. Everything, every form, has a center—its own personal resonance, its own heart. And that is the way it stays connected, by its own identifiable resonance. That is how it determines its essence and keeps its form. Thus, a plum tree produces plums, a cherry tree produces cherries.

The sun gives the plants energy made of inspiration, and this way they stay alive. The plants stay alive by breathing. They breathe in sunlight, and through photosynthesis they process it. That is how they produce their energies, their fruits.

Energy is constantly moving. The sun dancer knows this from breathing in and breathing out through the hollow bone. After a while, by virtue of doing this hundreds of times, and through years of practice, we learn that our breathing in and out is the same as the energy going from the Earth up to the sky and back down to the Earth, up to the sky and back down again.

At Picuris, they use the pole climb to show the same thing. In the pole climb, they go up the pole to get the things that are waiting at the top, and then they come down. Another example is the vertical line of the Christian cross. This ability to move up and down is an attribute that we get from the sun. This up-and-down-flowing energy bonds whatever is near with whatever is far away. It connects the finite with the infinite in this process of moving up and down.

When the finite self is connected to the infinite self, then the soul comes in. Soul is like the soil that gives sunlight a place to put down roots. Sunlight roots itself in soil, so that the plant can grow to its greatest quality. It gives some roots into the ground and it gives a sense of purity and clarity.

There is the dialog between the light and no-light, between day and night.

The daylight, philosophically, is the rational mind; everything that is knowable is light. Everything that is rational, that can be understood, has this clarity of the sunlight. The night is the creative.

The soil gives the plant the gift of manifestation, of movement, so that it can bond to the heavens. It is stuck in the ground with roots and it grows upward toward the sun, and in that process it is going up toward the heavens and bonding with them. Should that plant be in poor soil, it will not

Harvest
Belt
Dance

inspiration

116

Harvest Belt Dance

produce its highest potential. This also applies to the human condition. If we don't place ourselves in the rich soil of life that is nourishing to us, we may not achieve our potential.

When the Picuris people heard about the explosion of an atom bomb at Hiroshima, we performed a ceremony to bring about peace. We took all the implements of war from the village and buried them in the ground. The reason that we take a powerful instrument and stick it in the ground is to send it back to its origin, to the infinite self. The finite is the weapon, the infinite is the Earth. So we send it back. And when we send it back that way, something happens psychically to the planet and to the object. It returns to innocence—back to the Self—just like the image in the Bible of beating swords into plowshares. When we place something in the ground, the vibration of that object reverts to an energy of compassion.

The Picuris people, when they buried the weapons of war, were taking care of the Earth. They see theirs as a role of caretaking. Caretaking is what the shepherds were doing when Jesus was born.

When you put something in the ground, when you bury anything, it returns to the dream. When you bury a rifle, it returns back to the dream, before it was dreamt into rifle-ness for the purposes of injury, of killing.

Material Forms ≈ Crystallized forms, such as rocks, hold the energy of their connections to the upper planes, to the realm where inspiration comes from. They also carry the capacity to radiate energy. This energy wants to help the personal self as well as the infinite self by moving all things to climb. This energy asks to ascend; it moves things higher.

Everything, even the hard rock, is alive. Nothing is really inanimate. When you fast for days without food or water, you see the rock is really buzzing with life. Each rock is different. You can see the difference and you know which rock is a heart rock, which rock is a lung rock, which is a walking rock. It is not that you just pick up any rock and say, "This is a heart rock." Each rock resonates with a principal idea of oneness, heartness, sittingness, or walkingness. Each rock talks to you and tells you what it is.

Ordinary life is continually talking to us, but we eat too much salt and too much sugar. Salt in your body steals your light. It robs you of your capacity to see physically. You are less able to perceive accurately and quickly, and to comprehend what is perceived. When the salt level drops, it creates a resonance of craving, a vacuum that calls light into it. I've been doing sweat lodges (where my body loses salt through sweating) for forty years, and I know from personal experience that I can see better when my body is low on salt.

Sugar makes our blood cry. It gives us a craving and makes us jittery. We have no peace. We are too well fed, too full, too comfortable to hear life talking to us. We lose our capacities to connect. In fasting, we go back to the guiding advice of ordinary life, and we can learn from everyday things like stones, leaves, the bark of a tree, the bark of a dog.

One of the things the rock wants to do, one of its jobs, is to create linkages, connecting us not just to the finite, but to the infinite, the essence of our beingness. Because we are infinite. Of course, we are also finite. We can take a microscope and look down into the cells of our own bodies. That is the finite. But we are also part of the vastness of an infinite universe. I tried traveling the universe once and discovered that it went on for millions and millions and millions of light years. Actually it is round, like a beehive that goes on forever. Each one of its cells or circles is an eternity.

The universe is a whole philosophical perspective of the understanding. It is a vast working model of how the unfolding of consciousness is occurring, so that we have a cognitive as well as creative resonance or image. This unfolding of consciousness is occurring on the micro as well as the macro scale, so that every single action that is taken, whether it is mental, emotional, physical or spiritual, is in dialogue with this presence, with this understanding of cosmic truth.

josephrael.org/
fasting.mp3

inspiration

119

Climbing ≈ In Tiwa we say *weh-leh-who*, which means to climb upward. Remember every single word in Tiwa has multiple meanings; it is not just one thing. To the ordinary person in Picuris, when we say, *weh-leh-who*, that means "we climb upward." *Weh-leh-who* means we are now in a place of no judgment or control. We are not thinking about what is going to happen; we are totally innocent. We are teachable at that point. We are emptiness.

Leh means we become the essence of peace, the tool of peace, of connection to the vertical light of the Vast Self moving upward.

We use the word *leh-leh*, which means belt. *Leh* means the "belt of peace." (That is where the wampum belt comes from.) Imagine a belt around my middle. I want to slip that belt up to a higher charka. The word, the sound vibration *lay*, is there. It means you bring the belt from the lower charka up, for new understanding.

A belt is not just to keep your clothes on. The belt line area of the physical anatomy of the human being is telling us to move higher. When someone used the word *leh-leh* at Picuris, that used to tell us, "You slouch. There is no reason why you have to walk as if you were walking down a blind alley anymore. You can be enlightened. You can know that a belt is more than a belt." So the second meaning, the fuller understanding of this belt, is that it is to give us purity, higher clarity. It is the potential to connect the personal self to the pathway between that which is physical and that which is spiritual. So now we can cross freely back and forth between where we happen to be physically at this moment in time and space and where God is. God can feed us inspiration because we have a corridor, a pathway. It is like the hollow bone, where energy comes thorough freely up and down, and gives us enlightenment.

The interesting thing about this realm, this corridor, is that it is open only for a short time, maybe a split second, or maybe three seconds or five seconds. Then it shuts down again and waits for you to apply yourself mentally, emotionally,

Climbing
and
crossing
between
Worlds
ceremony

inspiration

120

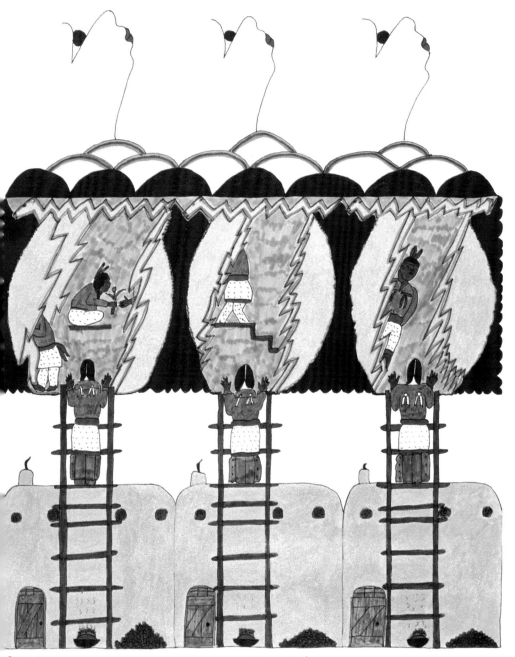

Climbing and crossing between Worlds ceremony

physically, or spiritually. Or, more likely, you apply yourself in all those ways because they tend to happen together. Through effort, the self goes back up to the top and it opens up, gets more inspiration, then brings this inspiration back down again.

Effort that is applied when doing physical tasks is a necessity in daily life because it is that work effort that escapes the physical world into the invisible field. It waits there for us to call upon its gifts to humanity. Then, when it is needed, it returns to replenish physical energy on the Earth. Prayer is the form I use to bring the effort energy back from the invisible realms to heal planet Earth.

When I talk about how we are learning to be, I sometimes put it in terms of the equidistant cross. When we are at the bottom of the cross, we are like water. We flow to the lowest place, we find the lowest common denominator.

Now, as soon as we apply effort, we begin to lift ourselves up until we reach up to the highest potential. This is the only time when we truly exist. That is when we are having an impact, when we are contributing something to humanity.

The rest of the time we are being in the normal vibration, which is in the middle—or maybe we are not even reaching that. We are basically kind of lazy, but through effort we move ourselves to normalcy, which is the middle, and then, as we go up higher, we are better and better and better, but we are still not at our fullest potential.

inspiration

Our fullest potential comes when we get a flash of light. We reach a peak experience at which point we've broken through to a new level of being, a new level of understanding, a new level of cognizance, a new level of awareness. We have touched the source of our inspiration, the source that has given the physical body life.

1??

Think of a cross with a horizontal bar and a vertical bar. The horizontal bar is the personal self. That is the rational self that says, this is what life is, all the different forms. "I had better not walk in front of a moving car, I might get run over." That is the personal self. Now, the vertical part of the cross is the Vast Self. As the horizontal bar moves up, it is being fed by the heavenly planes, which are out to the left and the right of the vertical bar. These heavenly planes are feeding the consciousness with inspiration. The self is fed, but not yet enlightened. The only time it is enlightened is when it has achieved its true potential through effort. That is when a light comes on and you feel totally washed with light.

Fasting ≈ Fasting has always been used to enhance this process: to enhance faith, to clarify our thinking about doctrine or values, and thus to increase belief. How does this work on the vibrational level?

First of all, in its original state the energy that creates all form—concrete or abstract—is rapidly moving light energy. This energy slows down to a crawl so that it becomes matter. The light slows to become physical forms—atoms and molecules. Inside matter, however, imagine that the energy remains moving, now in slow motion, just barely in a state of movement, so that it can't be perceived by the human at all.

When the person fasts, his psychic energy begins to speed up, evoking precognitive dreams, premonitions, or instructive visionary experiences. By speeding up the psychic flow of energy, fasting increases the energy of the normal human intelligence, giving birth to a new awareness. The old pattern changes, changing the behavior of the person.

Faith is enhanced in three ways. First there remains an increased awareness that was not there before, and because of this a pattern has changed. Secondly, a greater freedom is experienced. Third, there is a renewed interest in one's life, an increased desire to contribute to life, which is the essence of faith.

In summary, fasting changes the slow-moving flow of the person's human intelligence and speeds it up to a rapid pace, which allows for paranormal experiences and enhanced faith.

Rapidly moving light energy is the hunter, stalking knowledge. *Chueh-lo* is speed in Tiwa. *Chueh-lo* hunts and captures the form that is to be rooted or placed.

Pii-aah-saah is slow motion in Tiwa. Slow motion places

Dream Catcher

and roots life as a form. Slowly moving light energy—matter on the physical level—is constantly being purified with heart energy.

Movement ≈ In Tiwa, goodness and movement are synonymous.

Fasting, prayer, and meditation are incorporated in some movement or action—good action. Many of the ancient mystery schools and monasteries of ancient times encouraged fasting and prayer, because the basis for reaching one's highest potential is prayerful meditation, which is a spiritual movement.

Now movement is also what gives us the capacity to perceive. Without movement it is as if we have been born without eyes. We have no eyes to see with and no inner eye— the third eye.

Movement is an essential part of God-ness on this plane of reality, because God is breath, matter, and movement. Without movement, there cannot be creation in matter. Without movement, the breath cannot instill creativity. It is that movement that helps us see that we can create the next thing. Without movement, we can't see what is being created. And that is why we have materialization into form—so that we can see. Seeing, perceptual reality, and material form are the same.

Placement ≈ Everything in the natural material world exists to tell us and to show us how well we are doing.

For instance, *cha* is the tree. *Cha* is also the now. *Cha* is the tree of life and *cha* is greatness. If you were to fast seven or eight days, as soon as you touched a tree or you sat on it or leaned on it, it would tell you how much greatness is there. That is in the vibration, *cha*. That vibration might tell you that you could be doing better. It might tell you to consider your age and the effort you're putting into life. It might also teach you how you can continue to keep yourself in greatness, because that is in its vibration.

In the same way, when you have been fasting for a few

inspiration

125

days without food or water, a heart stone is going to connect you to where your center is. It will show you the God-given gifts that you were born with, that make up your center, your resonance. Even as a plum tree produces a plum and a cherry tree produces a cherry, so you are born with the capacity to produce your own particular form of fruit. Each entity or each form has to go back to its resonance to check in, to find out what it is being. Since we are mental, emotional, physical, spiritual beings, we go back to find our placement.

That is why Native American practices are so popular today. People really want to find themselves again; they really want to find their placement, so they go to a culture that has kept these ceremonies. But we are so connected to form that we look at a dance and say, "Oh, what a great rattle. It has this horsehair on it. It has these beads on it." We get distracted from the core, resonant vibration that this ceremony is about.

The ceremony is really there to get us in touch with something in ourselves that makes up the constellation of our presence here. When we really connect to these different ceremonies—not so much to their appearances, but to their mystical resonances, their vibrations—we can get in touch with the core essence of that particular form, that particular understanding.

Weh-leh-who ≈ *Weh-leh-who* means to go up. *Weh* means to give. *Leh* means the horizontal plane. *Who* gives us a sense of being carried. It gives us a sense of the connection to the vastness, to the heavenly planes. *Who* means God is carrying us, or God is carrying the action that is being taken. This is connecting us to the highest potential of the heavenly planes, and it is giving us the place of childlike innocence in which we are simply conduits of energy at the core of existence—energy that is moving through us without any effort on our part and nourishing our souls.

This doorway to the core stays open only long enough to present insight, and then it closes down and waits for the next input of psychic energy. We are like strobe lights; we go off and on and off and on. Our movements, as we act out these insights through effort, create the next opening, a corridor to new insights and inspirations.

Walking in beauty ≈ So how do we keep ourselves open to insights? By treating ourselves and others as we would like to be treated.

In Tiwa, goodness means *co-wen*. It means the beauty of childlike innocence, loving kindness that is climbing upwards through the base self, more and more becoming new beauty. *Co-wen* in everyday speech means "all is well," but it really means all is well because what is being enhanced is beauty. All beauty wants is more beauty, and the person's attitude is right. That person is in the right place, because he is really only being beauty. That is all he chooses to be—the highest potential of beauty that he can be at this point.

Beauty is the only thing we are here for. In everything else we do, we are just trying to find beauty.

The three essentials to be in a state of beauty are:

LEVEL 1: You have to have that connection with Oneness;

LEVEL 2: You have to be in reflection (which is what we call duality):

LEVEL 3: You have to be in movement.

Beauty is the action of being in the moment. In the moment, you cannot solely be at level number one. You have to simultaneously be on levels two and three. I think that's what they mean by the Holy Trinity, the Three-in-One.

In Tiwa, beauty is *bah-chu*. *Bah* is related to the legs. The word *chu* means everywhere. When you are in the state of beauty, you are everywhere but nowhere. But you are in a state of movement, which is beauty that has connected to all the heavenly planes and is being carried by God. You are in a state of beatitude.

When the Native American people speak of walking in beauty, they're really saying, "Walk in love." This is the blessing way.

Four Winds, Elders of the sacred Blessing Way

One of the qualities of the blessing way is the connection that we have with the people that we love, our fellow human beings. What we need to do is keep a loving bond between us. Then we realize that if we have a loving bond with plants, animals, and the land around us, as if we were in a garden and we were the gardener, then we walk in beauty, and the beauty is who we are and what we are doing. Beauty comes from our relationship to all those around us.

At the end of their prayers, the Indians say, "All my relations." That's what they're talking about. We have a bond. Bonding is one of the qualities of Beauty.

Beauty is also purity. And what is purity? Purity exists when the heart fuses with carrying. We carry each other; we carry our philosophies. That is one of the qualities of purity, an awareness that crystallizes in this radiance of inner knowing so that we can see the spiritual and the physical connection.

One of the things purity is doing in the context of beauty is crystallizing, so that we can see, so that we can feel and then have a clarity of the connection between inspiration and materialism. Beauty is seeing something that is manifesting and that is clear, has intent, has purity, and that gives us a special insight about inspiration.

The last aspect of beauty is awareness. In the true experience of beauty, awareness is total. The true experience of beauty is to disappear into those qualities that I have just spoken about. When you disappear into them, you have no desire for them. You just *are* them. That is what our prayer says when it speaks of the beauty path to the four directions.

The beatitudes of life are to celebrate how it is that we are walking here. Walking is the way we celebrate our toes, and our feet, and our legs, and our backs, and our eyes, and our hands, and our arms, and all of our internal organs. Because everything is in movement. Walking in beauty is an orchestration of all of the beatitudes—the holy walk in this plane.

inspiration

Ah-who ≈ Think again of the cross. When the horizontal bar is at the top of the vertical line, that is the only time we are doing anything that is worthwhile. It is at the moment that we are taking a brand new action when we are reaching the highest potential. This is the moment when the old pattern dies, when God comes in and is involved in our actions. Now, we are the physical body for the translation of that energy into our next highest potential. This is the moment of transformation for us as the actors in liaison with God's presence. And the transformation is not just for us: At that moment, we are also enhancing cosmic consciousness. In Tiwa, we say whenever we are doing something worthwhile, we are contributing to the basic humanity of that moment in history.

The Picuris people are very intelligent beings, and I think it is because they follow this doctrine. Whether they know it or not, it is innate in their language. They say "*Ah who.*" *Ah who* means "the breath of highest inspiration is washing us."

ah-who

inspiration

Tiwa is not concerned about two-leggeds, or four-leggeds, or any particular species. Its only interest is achievement of the highest potential, the highest energy level of purity, so the soul can be fed. In this way, we imprint the future and promote the evolution of unconditional love in consciousness.

The Indians signed contracts with the government to provide them with all of their needs—their social, economic, and political needs. That created a dependency. And with dependency, people don't try to excel. Instead of exploding to new consciousness, they begin to implode. I found in my research that dependency creates a lot of alcoholism and drug abuse, because people are not happy. They are not trying to achieve their highest potential.

Again, good action takes place when God is doing the action. Any time we are doing something good, God is there, because God is the being who is achievement. Goodness comes into being through our actions. The actions that we take together with God bring us physical satisfaction and fulfill our longing for life.

Life by its very nature is a giant church made of

ah-who

unconditional love, a place where the soul is continually fed. Whenever you practice your highest potential, you are feeding the soul what it needs. You are keeping yourself open with inspirational thoughts. Then you feel great, and you jump up and say, "Wow! This is great stuff!"

Truly, all there is in life is beauty made of unconditional love and everything else we do is simply a time of waiting for beauty to happen again and again.

When I say we don't exist, I mean that the only time we truly exist is when we are reaching and being our highest potential. We are at the top of the vertical bar. At any other time, we are not contributing either to ourselves or to humanity. We are simply existing. When we are simply existing, that is when we get into activities like killing each other, because we are not happy. We are not happy because we are just existing. We ask for the death of this pattern in which we are stuck so we may be reborn into the breath of inspired living.

Yet, we humans are afraid of dying. This fear arises because we are separate from the Vast Self. But we have separated to find out what it means to be separate form, so that we could understand that the false code of materialism is not what God is. God is relationship to eternal life.

Matter and miracles ≈ Through life in this material dimension, we carry on a dialogue with materialism. This dialogue automatically puts us in touch with how materialism is inspiring us to create more of what matters in our lives.

God brings two powers together—the material and the eternal. When this happens, then we can do what some people call the miraculous.

The miraculous, interestingly enough, only appears on the scene during times of emergency. During an emergency, we somehow merge that part of our separate selves back to true Self. In that moment—in that flash of light—we can manifest our true essence.

An emergency occurs when the world we have created has

collapsed. What we perceive as the "real world" is really just a collection of things we have constructed in our psyche that we understand to be reality. When that reality is shattered—in that instant—our self-assurance ends. And at that point, we truly exist.

The rest of the time, we don't exist. The rest of the time we are trying to establish we exist.

We try to establish we exist by perpetuating our various perceptions of reality. We are afraid that if we don't, we will disappear; and that if we disappear, we will die; and that if we die, we don't exist; not realizing that we really *don't* exist. Then we give it up, and we shatter our reality in the split of the moment. Only then are we really in touch with the Vast Self. Only then do we really exist.

Maybe it happens during an earthquake, when all of a sudden trees and houses are falling down, when the freeway is cracking open and swallowing cars. At that moment, you give up. Then all of a sudden you are out of the danger; you are way over on the other side of the mountain. Your mind says, "Hey, what happened? I must have just thought I was in danger." No, you really were in danger, but a miracle happened automatically because destiny decided that it needed you for another week.

So, our technological mastery of the universe is proper in order to find out that it is not mastery of anything. It is mastery of self, which is not really mastery of anything. It is how we come to know that we just simply *are*.

Innocence and awe ≈ All our efforts and technology are ways we purposefully veer away from our center. We do it because, in the expansion of the vastness, we have an innocence in us that is extremely curious. Innocence is curious, just like a little child. It wants to look at everything, and then after awhile it becomes awestruck by what it sees and begins to make gods of those things.

It is so awestruck that all of a sudden the date to the high school prom is the most wonderful thing that has happened in the whole universe and—*gee!*—the lights will never end, and you've arrived in heaven and you are glad you veered away from the center to have this experience.

My Tiwa grandfather taught me that work is worship. And yet if we don't exist, and none of this exists, and there is nothing that we really need to do except know that we don't exist (except in the sense that we are part of the Vast Self), why do we need to work?

We need to work because we have physical bodies, and these physical bodies are really forms that can be traced back to sacred dimensions. In perceptual, material reality, the sacred dimensions finally end up looking like a finger on a hand. In that finger, in that hand, these sacred dimensions are present, and every time we move the finger, every time we are in the state of movement, we are worshiping the finger idea. Work is worship. By movement, or work, we keep this body strong so that we can continue worshiping that original idea of the finger, or the back, or the knees, or the feet.

A microcosm of the Vast Self ≈ The human is the microcosm of all that is contained in the macrocosm of the Vast Self. The words given for the parts of the body in Tiwa tell us what principal ideas we are worshiping as we move and use each part.

The ear in Tiwa is *tlschu*, which means *to do in order to give*.

The face is *tzu*, which means *to enter*.

The skin is *hai*, which means *to lift*.

The head is *peh-nay*, which means *to focus*.

Hair is *pah*, which means *light*.

Clothing is *pii ah*, which means *to make*.

The tongue is *wn-men*, which means *giving to awareness*.

The eyes are *cheh*, which means *to cook*.

The nose is *pwfu-ii*, which means *to expand*, and also *to pin onto*.

The mouth is *tschlah moh*, which means *to see greatness*.

The feet are *iin*, which means *placement*.

The legs are *bahh*, which means *direction*, the direction in which something is to go.

Hands are *maa-nay-nay*, which means *to manifest*, or *to create*.

The arms are *haah-eh*, which means *to embrace*.

The body as a whole is *tu-nay*, which means *beauty*. When we work with our bodies, we are worshiping the principal idea of beauty, as well as the principal ideas of all its parts.

In order to keep worshiping, we have to keep working our bodies. Thus, we create institutions around work, and then we throw in something like money as a motivator. Whenever the human moves, whatever he does, he is already in ceremony. She is already in ceremony. Each ceremony that we perform is to help us remember the ceremony that we *are*. It is to further enhance our relationship to the vastness of who we are. We are the original cosmic plan that eventually, as it came into being, took on human form.

We are catalysts, here to bring about changes. When we walk, we are balancing left and right. With each step, we move too far off in one direction and we have to balance by coming back to the other direction.

Sometimes we lose our balance entirely. What our bodies are telling us at that moment when there is discomfort or stress is that there is a state of evolution that is occurring—physical evolution. Something new is being programmed into the biological system. Perhaps it won't manifest itself for another seven hundred years, but something is being transformed.

We are a tiny model of the bigger picture. Maybe I've been working to get something done and it is not getting done, so I'm frustrated. I want to yell; maybe I do yell, and I feel guilty. When that is going on in my microcosm, in the macrocosm, maybe five or six solar systems away, I've created a definite shift in consciousness.

We are consciousness ≈ We humans are made up of all of the eternities, so when something is going on out there, it is reflecting back here. The discomfort we are feeling here is reflecting what is going on out there.

This is a very Indian (Native American) idea. Whenever we are dancing or having a ceremony, we know we are not just doing it for us. We are doing it for the larger being, of which we are a microcosm.

I am totally convinced that what we are doing here is exactly what we came here to do. We just keep doing it and we know that we are affecting some other dimensions because of our work here. This happens because we have these physical bodies that are not really just flesh and blood and bone, but are actually Principal Ideas. We were created so that we could function here, so that we could play a role in the unfolding of all the multiple dimensions of wisdom and truth. This unfolding is happening because of what our physical anatomy is doing.

We were given a mind to think as part of an inducement for being here.

One of the things I've found out about human beings is that nothing can harm us. Certainly someone can kill us and they can torture us, but they can't really rub us out because we are set on this vibration that goes on and on forever and we just keep showing up in different places. We do not simply *have* consciousness; we *are* consciousness.

Symbols ≈ In order to understand how consciousness works, we have to understand that symbols are themselves vibrations. When we see a line that is going up and down or is going horizontally in a letter of the alphabet, we have to know that those horizontal and vertical lines have power in and of themselves. We use symbolic letters, or symbolic forms like numbers, because they have mystical power. Numbers have resonating vibrations. The cosmos is made of three things: numbers, letters, and sounds. We are made up of numbers, letters, sounds.

Mother
Nature of
fields and
Streams
A child of
innocence
born in
every
moment

inspiration

136

corn field

Streams

innocence

a cloak of feathers

Mother Nature
Of fields and Streams
A Child of innocence born in every moment

(c) 2003 Joseph Beautiful Painted Arrow

The cosmos is created by symbols. When you combine planting and seeing, those together become a sound vibration—a symbol.

In the vastness of *ooh*, in that innocence, there are some qualities. One of those is *naa-peh-cho*, which means numbers.

Naa is to manifest. *Naa-peh-cho* gives us focus, direction, lineage, a target. That is what the head is created from. In the physical anatomy of the human body, the head is numberness. Numbers are the reason that we appear with a head, or that anything appears with a head. The head is the first. It guides. The head of a movement is the one who guides the movement.

Naa-peh-cho: Naa brings into existence, and *peh* is preciseness. It is like the arrowhead or the head of a movement; it is leadership. It is very important that we have that precision or clarity, that we master and understand that focus.

Cho means everywhere—*and then some!*

Cho is childlike innocence, connecting us to all other planes.

Again, *Naa* is to bring manifestation into existence. *Peh* means directions, focus. *Cho* means beauty that connects us to all the heavenly things.

Numbers came into existence to open the corridor to high states of being.

The letters on the other hand have to do with *cah-naa*, which means how the Self is designing itself on the surface of being. Letters are imprinting what *naa-peh-cho* is trying to say; letters are imprinting what that movement is designating.

And sound is *poh*, which means the status quo. It means how the heart sees itself in relationship to the original circle of light. How the divine heart, the divine centeredness, or loving-kindness is in relationship to the original design.

So now, with numbers, letters and sounds together, you have the head of a family—the head of a focus—that has imprinted itself within this medicine wheel, so that it knows what it is.

As we learn more of our relationship with our heart and our intent, which is the focus of numerology, and our sense of knowing, because it is imprinted within our psyche, we can get out of the wheel. The only thing that gets us out is personal enlightenment, and then universal enlightenment. At that point, however, as soon as we kick out of this wheel, guess what? We just go next door. We get into another circle. There are millions and millions of these circles.

Chanting ≈ We want to go beyond the ordinary through chanting, through singing. We get stuck in the materialization; we are too materialistic, so that most of the unhappiness on the planet is the result of the soul not receiving its nourishment. When you go into ceremony through chanting, you bring time and future or past orientation into *cha*, which means *now* and which also means *song*. In order to feed the soul, you have to come into the here and now. In truth, the here and now does not exist, only Divine Love that looks and feels like the here and now.

Chanting puts your attention back into the very present. If you really concentrate on chanting, you are not thinking about what you are going to do tomorrow or what you did last year. You *are* the actual chanting itself. Eventually, you can transcend the five vowel vibrations and go into an altered state or parallel reality.

You can do this more easily with a group than as an individual. The group vibration is all around you and it is impinging on your physical body. Your body is like a vibratory instrument. It is vibrating, and group chanting enhances this. Group chanting magnifies the effect because the whole body is feeling the vibration of many voices impinging upon it. The whole psyche then reverts to beauty that is completing new moments of clarity. We are singing clarity into rightful living.

Native Americans are present-oriented. The languages they speak are present-oriented, because to remain present-oriented is to access these alternate realities that we are talking about. This present orientation keeps you moving and keeps you alive and connected.

Singing or chanting does something very special with time as it places the seeds of our aspirations into the framework of a future time and place. Most ceremonies in cultures all over the world use singing and chanting. This is because chanting in ceremony creates a pathway for beauty and awareness to merge into one essence.

As we start chanting, beauty, which has the physical properties of movement and cold, begins to heat up. Heat, which is ancientness, begins to flow into the cold of beauty, and as soon as this happens, the ceremony begins to move the cold truth from the ground level upward, toward a higher purity. This movement can be explained as heat pushing from the floor level upward to the ceiling. Hot air penetrates the cold air as it rises, taking us to higher points of illumination.

As the truth rises and purifies, our intention in doing the ceremony is being carried into the future where it will be realized. For example, let us say that we are doing the ceremony in March for better crops in the summer. As we chant, that beauty rises, merges awareness with heat, and we become aware of a new illumination, which can now be realized in the material realm.

Chanting affects our bodies on a cellular level and it affects all the Earth and plants as well. It clears away blocks so that life energy can flow uninterrupted; it frees stuck energy in the physical world around us.

Chanting also brings new energy from the heavens, from the realm of pure ideas, into the biosphere. Everything in the biosphere is the result of principal ideas that lie latent in the realm of pure undifferentiated light-like energy and come to Earth for materialization. Chanting connects us with those principal ideas and helps bring them into form.

Plants do not just grow up from the ground searching for sunlight. The realm of pure ideas is pulling the plants up into itself. These principal ideas take material form as plants in order to embody something that has been latent in the there all along. Chanting helps this process by unblocking their life energies and connecting them to the new vibrations from that

Watermelon
Plant people
making food
for the
children of
Mother Earth

inspiration

140

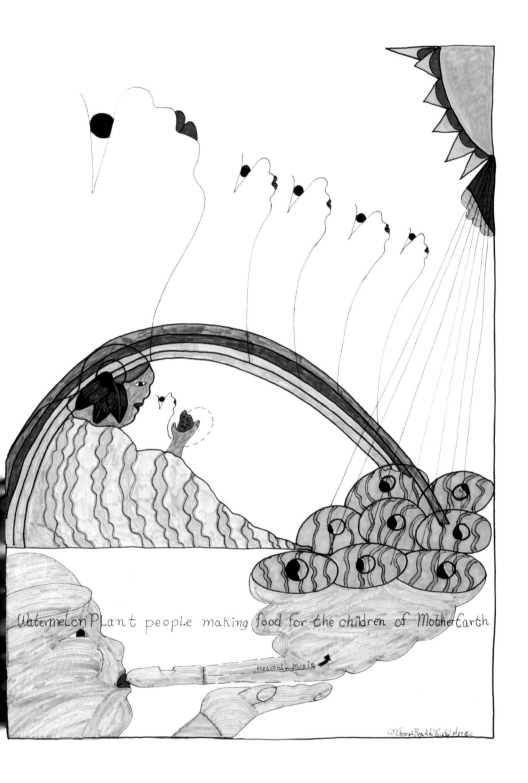

realm of light-like energies. We are the environment creating more environments for us to live into.

In Tiwa belief, there is a direct connection between our conscious illuminations or thoughts and what our future experiences will be. By making a conscious connection with the new energies and principal ideas that are latent in the realms of light, we form a bridge between the heavens and the Earth, and between the present and the future. In the singing part of the ceremony, the chanting creates a premonition of some future time by creating the future in the here-and-now time frame. In chanting, we plant the here-and-now with seeds of our intentions for the future.

Realm of magic ≈ I believe that the different ceremonies that have been done through the centuries were done because people were trying to find the space that I call the realm of magic — white magic — where you create in a positive way the environment that will enhance the continuation of life in the physical body. For instance, if you are chanting and someone is being healed, that singing enables the person to get well because, at some point, the body of the person who is being healed merges with the parallel reality in that other realm so that the doctor can reach in and heal the sickness. It can be healed because these two worlds have merged. Through ceremony, we bring the two worlds into coexistence. That is where we can access the future, which exists in the parallel reality.

Normal reality is based on separation, which produces fear. The realm of white magic is based on love. When we bring the two together, love can transform fear into healing potential.

A holy person can do this at will. Now what we want is for everybody to be able to do this when they choose to do it.

The culture of the United States is where it is because it is seeking a way by which to continue enhancing states of union. This is a way to carry the culture in order to enhance the beauty. The original idea was good, but it doesn't always end up that way. The direction twists. That is the reason we have technology moving too fast now, creating things faster than we can use them or digest them.

Technology is moving so fast because a couple of hundred years ago, we cut down too many trees. How would cutting too many trees affect technology? The metaphor or the vibration of greatness is connected to trees. When we cut the trees, they fall to the Earth. Like the feminine energy that falls from the heavenly sphere into the biosphere where it manifests new material forms, the trees go from the vertical to the horizontal plane. This causes a different energy in the biosphere, creating more things at a faster rate. The trees have the sky energy, and when the sky energy falls, it jumps back up and it falls back down. It awakens receptivity and creates activity. As the trees hit the Earth and bounce, the culture becomes more active. We create more technology, the population booms, wars erupt. All those things come from frenetic energy, caused by the cutting down of trees.

Indian thinking says: when you do something, be careful; because what you do is going to have side effects. It is not just cutting down trees; it is changing the whole energetic configuration of the culture. That is why we do ceremonies. They can contribute to the shifts in consciousness for a culture within a geography. When we do ceremonies, we are working on the energies.

The true visionary knows that the original idea of any ceremony came from a vision. The vision told the person who received it everything that needed to be done in the ceremony, so there was absolutely no guesswork. When I get a vision, I am told exactly, step by step, how to do it, and if I don't do it right then there are angels, or beings, that come from the other side and tell me I made a mistake.

Once you agree to be a visionary, the above beings give you a vision and you have to do it; you can't say no. Once we have decided to come to this Earth, we have to live up to certain criteria, because what we are doing has a direct connection to what is going on in the other dimensions. Each of us came here as the result of a vision. The planet had a vision, and as a

inspiration

143

result of that, you happened and I happened. Once the planet had a vision, then we came as a result of divine calling, divine longing. So we agreed to come down, and by the time we were born we had already been given a place on the planet. We were born to fulfill that vision. All the trials and tribulations are exercise. Their purpose is to make us the best possible conduits to move energy through the world, to enhance creation. We come here to manifest. We come to live in the world of illusion, to be in states of awe.

It is possible for ceremonies to become empty of their power. If you continue to follow the original prescription, the process of a ceremony, the same form over and over, it will empty the ceremony. Yet there is a good reason for purists. They know that you have to do the ceremony right if you are in this ordinary reality. Now once you get out of ordinary reality, the form doesn't matter. Once you are connected to the realm of magic in which you have the potential of all of these vibrations, purity is no longer an issue for you. Nor is placement, awareness, carrying or innocence. You only have to deal with them insofar as where you happen to be at the time. Am I pure enough, or clear enough to move in this realm?

So I think we first have to learn the concrete sense of carrying, placement, and innocence before we can appreciate the reality where we will no longer need them. Ceremony is to help us, by using these forms, and as we work through them,

they put us in the place where the forms no longer matter. We go from concreteness into abstractness and from abstractness back into concreteness—from parallel reality to normal reality—until they finally merge.

We are trying to live in the present tense, totally here but totally in a space of paradise where the two are simultaneously

occurring. That is achieved only when we work at it by continually purifying ourselves. Ceremony is the way to do this. It gives us these powers. Ceremony works because it is crying for a vision. By crying for a vision, I mean that the soul is longing for light, so it can drink the light and thus fulfill its nature. If light—vision—is lacking, there is sadness.

There are a lot of sad people in our world. People may have an abundance of material things, but they still lack deep inner satisfaction. We can get fulfillment when we go to church for communion, or into the sweat lodge, or to a ceremony of some type. The ceremony heals the loneliness, fulfils the longing, and allows universal intelligence to come in.

The sweat lodge ≈ Native people almost always do sweat lodges before other ceremonies, as a purification and a preparation. This is because we need to program our minds, we have to program our bodies so that when we go into the ceremony we can maximize what we are going to get out of it.

To do the ceremony, a sweat lodge is framed out with willow poles lashed together to create a domed, circular enclosure. The willows are covered with blankets or tarps, making it completely dark inside the lodge. Lava rocks are heated red-hot in a bonfire outside the lodge. In the ceremony, people crawl into the lodge and sit in a circle around a pit in the earth at the center of the hut. Then a helper uses a pitchfork to lift the heated rocks one by one from the fire and drop them in the pit inside the lodge. The tarp is pulled over the doorway. Then water is poured on the rocks and hot steam fills the lodge. Sage and other sweet-smelling herbs are also sprinkled on the burning rocks, filling the lodge with beautiful aromas. Prayers are given honoring the four directions, one in each of four rounds. Between rounds the tarp is raised, cooling the air inside the sweat lodge. More hot rocks are taken from the fire and placed in the sweat lodge pit and then the door-flap is closed again. With the door closed, the inside of the sweat lodge is completely dark and gets very hot so people are soon covered with sweat. The sweating itself is purification on a physical level, but even more powerful things happen on the psychic and spiritual levels.

When I'm going to build the sweat lodge, the first thing I do is dig the pit where the rocks are going to go when we bring them from the fire and put them in the center of the lodge. What I do is take the earth from that hole in the middle of the sweat lodge and I put it on the right hand side of the doorway (as you are facing in) to make a shrine where people can put things. The pile of dirt that has come from the center of the sweat lodge is heart energy. The shrine is made out of the heart, so whatever we put on the shrine gets blessed. On the shrine people might put their eyeglasses in order to receive better vision, or they might put, symbolically, a relative that needs healing. Or they might put a medicine bag there or they might put a peace pipe there—anything they want blessed.

Then when I'm building the sweat lodge I place the upright willows about a foot and a half apart in each of those four directions, east, south, west and north, so that the lodge will be oriented in the cardinal directions. The door of the lodge is on the west. Fourteen feet west of the door of the lodge, I dig a pit for the fire. The dirt taken from the fire pit I line out in a semicircle on the west side of the fire pit so it is like a reflector. The mound reflects firelight back toward the sweat lodge.

Before I build a fire in the fire pit, I put in the rocks. I get rocks that are smaller than football size. Usually I use about eighteen sweat lodge rocks for a sweat. I start by putting a rock to the east side of the fire pit, then one to the south and one to the west side of the pit and one to the north. Then I put one on to represent the above direction, one to represent the below direction. Then I fill in the half-directions and the rest of the circle and stack them on top of each other.

Another thing I do is make a line of corn meal from the fire pit to the pit in the sweat lodge. I connect the fire pit to the heart of the sweat lodge in order to make a trail for the stone people to come along that path where the corn meal is into the other pit inside the lodge. Corn meal is the symbol of awareness.

What is going on in the sweat lodge? The heat is a metaphor for ancientness. When we feel the intensity of the heat, it affects our bodies, heating our skin. As soon as the heat hits our skin, we get lifted. This response is in the genetic

Creator
of ocean
mist
always
brings
new
wisdom to
Learn

inspiration

Creator of ocean mist always brings new wisdom to Learn

code. Our bodies know we can go to a higher vibration; we can transcend everyday reality and reach the parallel reality. So we overheat the body. At some point, the heat will have to come down. The body will try to cool itself. At that break point, at the space between heating and cooling, illumination enters. There is a burst of energy, like a drop of water in a hot frying pan, and in that instant the light comes.

The salt we have in our bodies affects this process. Sweating a little, maybe for five minutes—gets the salt and sugar out, so we can achieve that state.

The top of the sweat lodge is a metaphor for the galaxies; that is where the sacraments come together. It is a focal point. The rocks symbolize the Earth and the first matter within the Earth, the lava. Water, which is a metaphor for light, becomes steam as it strikes the hot rocks, and the steam in that context is the power of the rock emerging. This is the power of the Earth Mother and the Sky Father coming together. Steam is releasing the energy of the stone.

In the interaction between coldness and heat we have the process of evolution. We have movement and time. Ancient wisdom is the summer, movement is the winter. When we put movement with ancient wisdom we have a manifestation of matter, or some orientational formulation of mental, emotional, physical, spiritual energies.

Ceremony, effort and survival ≈ Hot is "oldness" that is filled with awareness, and purifies by burning the veil between the ancient wisdom and the here-and-now. In a sweat lodge, the intense heat heats up our bodies. This brings a shift in consciousness. Heat puts us in touch with ancient wisdom. When the heat of ancient wisdom encounters cold awareness, there is movement, merging, and this creates a premonition that is to be acted upon. We now have the ability to see all the eternities that create potential possibility.

The ceremony awakens through focus and movement, using the productive force of nature, and implants our reality by programming into the future a given expected result. Actually, both the future and the past are here in the present, but they are in a parallel reality. Ceremony brings the ancient past into the present so we can learn from it. And ceremony also brings the future into the here-and-now and imprints it. Within intent is the energy to imprint the future. As soon as the chant or ceremony is over, the future goes back to the parallel reality and waits for us to show up five or six months later.

The planet eats the effort we expend, our prayers, sacred chanting, group worship, or our exertion in physical work. This is what the planet lives on.

Just as the heat of the sun on the surface of the Earth creates humidity that rises to form rain clouds, the heat of our prayers, chants, or physical effort rises into the realm of pure ideas, where our thoughts and ideas ferment into our next earthly experience. These ideas become actions to be taken by us humans.

All our new discoveries and inventions start at this level before they descend into our conscious minds. It is the effort that we place on our daily attempts to reach our highest physical, mental, emotional, and spiritual potential that the planet uses to survive.

It is the role of the adult to try to keep the firm stability of the status quo going on so that the children can have available to them the solid foundation to build upon. It is the role of the children as they become old enough to contribute to the planet to apply a certain amount of effort to make their new ideas known. This effort the children put out in order to succeed is what the planet eats.

The Earth, in its survival mode, will enhance any new ideas the child might seek to implement on the planetary scene. This is because the Earth plans with us every new thing we do here. Whatever we do today will affect the seventh generation down the line.

When you do a vision quest, it is a way to feed the soul. You merge back into the soul—this idea of *chai ka*. *Chai ka* means to plant a seed, and the seed creates life. *Ka* also means to dream. (*Ka* also means buffalo, and buffalo is a metaphor for

Mother Earth

Celestial Smudging Dish

Sage Woman becomes visible to - bless "the People"

the four pillars of truth that are dreaming states that make up the reflective universe we know as perceptual reality, which is illusionary.)

In this dream of material reality, we eat to stay alive, and other things are eating us to stay alive. Life, death, rebirth … all are part of this paradigm, this realm, this dream. In the ceremony, at some point, we go beyond this realm. It is no longer applicable.

Aroma ≈ When a holy person or a visionary teacher dies, he comes back and teaches his students in their dreams and enters their intuitive knowing. I think my grandfather stayed around for a while. Twenty years after his death, I received an illumination that carried his imprint; I could smell him. He had a smell like rose petals. I could identify him with that smell by the time I was five or six years old. Many years after he died, I was still getting teachings from him—insights—and when they would come I could smell my grandfather's scent of rose petals.

That is also how I remember my foster mother. She really loved red roses, and I gave her sixteen red roses when she was very sick. I had just gotten out of graduate school, and I walked into her room with roses. I remember the smile on her face when I gave her them. The next day, she died. When I entered the house, I heard this voice say: "don't look to the right, but just go straight into the bathroom." As I went in, I smelled a very strong scent of roses.

Scents and aromas manifest by the purity of innocence that is connecting itself to the energy of relationships. They manifest by the power of loving connections. I pray for all my relatives when we are praying in the sweat lodge. I want love. I want good rain. I want abundance for all my relations. Aroma was created out of these particular powers, when they merged together. It was the merging of these resonating vibrations that put together the essence or meaning of aroma. The reason aromatherapy works is that it carries the power of purity and innocence made of loving-kindness.

Sage Woman becomes visible to – bless "the People"

inspiration

151

What is that power, the purity of innocence? It has to be lovely, because it is so sincere. Innocence doesn't want anything. It doesn't demand anything. It doesn't care whether it succeeds or not. It is just pure, and this aroma is pure innocence that has fused to the capacity to manifest connections, so that all things that exist may be blessed. The connection makes us true brothers and sisters. It is like love. Innocence connects itself to everything that is.

Aroma is a way of connecting to that aspect of everything that is childlike innocence. Aroma is another way to hear something through smell, or see something through smell. It is a calling; we follow a scent. That is why incense is used in ceremony. Everything in life is a metaphor for an idea, and an idea is God's presence in our lives.

Sage, for instance, creates the energy that is necessary for us to transcend and go into the depths of the inner self. Cedar doesn't do that; cedar has to do with the journey that we are on, the journey in this world, whereas the sage has more to do with inner work. So when we inhale the aroma, it connects us to these qualities.

Cooking and imprinting ≈ Everything is connected to something else by virtue of a shared principle idea. For instance, the idea behind perceptual reality and cooking is imprinting. The Tiwa pronunciation of *eye* is the sound "cheh." "Cheh" is also the word sound for *cook*. At the center of our spiritual galaxy our human power of perception gets conceived and broadcast, not only to our planet Earth and our galaxy, but to other galaxies as well. Perceptual reality and cooking are essentially the same; they come from the same principle idea, which has to do with imprinting.

The process of materialization is when an idea gets "cooked" into a perceivable reality. That is what the eyes do. They see something and they say, "It is mine, it belongs to me," and there is a heat that is sent out. The heat goes out, hits the form, changes it in some way and returns it to the perceiver so that now it belongs to perception.

How many principal ideas are there? There could be as many as seven or fewer. There isn't a list. Everything in this reality is but a reflection of something that is out there somewhere, that is a principal idea. There is falling, running, walking, dreaming, standing, lying down, growing; these can all be connected to principal ideas.

Somewhere something is holding the energy of growingness so that everything is growing here. Little children are growing, plants are growing, trees are growing, and the only time they don't grow is when there is too much *chi*, so that they go into the dream, go into the cold.

We should try to live our present lives as well as possible, because how we live now, how we treat people, and how we treat ourselves is what we will get in the future. Our actions are imprinting that band of light-like undifferentiated energy from which inspiration comes. We are putting something there that later on we are going to eat. We are cooking our future.

Because we live in the form world in which everything around us is form, after awhile we tend to think in terms of form. But actually, we are not forms, we are energies that are creating the forms. Then we begin to believe in the form, and we become the form. I can say I am a carpenter, or I'm a janitor, or I'm a housewife, or a publisher. Pretty soon, we take on the attributes of the role, but actually, we are formless. In order to find our place, our true place, we teach ourselves to go back to knowing that everything around us is a form, but it is a form that we have created on some level. It is us but in a different form—a different expression of us.

Gold, for instance, is the symbol of the beauty of light, of the Universal Intelligence. Myrrh is the vibration of how manifestation is carrying its resonance. Frankincense has to do with the way we initiate our faith through beauty. It was appropriate that gifts of gold, frankincense, and myrrh be given to Jesus, because Jesus, like gold, was beauty in action. I can understand why the alchemists were trying to turn things into gold, because gold is a metaphor for purifying the self. Beauty is like divine purpose that has a loving resonance with the All-that-is. Beauty is the focus for the resonance with All-that-is. It is carrying crystallized awareness.

I've spent all my life trying to explain actions with metaphors so that in time, if I can keep going, and practicing, and thinking this way, eventually the metaphor and the thing are going to merge and become one.

Water is used in many ceremonies because it has to do with light. The essence of water is blessing someone with light. For instance, when water is used in baptism, it connects all of the heavens with innocence; innocence and the heavens become one. And you can't improve on that concept! Water is all the heavenly planes coming in simultaneously at every level. It is all going on simultaneously with one drop of water on your forehead. When you get baptized, it is innocence and all the heavens, captured in water that is light.

When blood first began to flow in the anatomy of beingness it was saying "yes" to light. Beingness could now manifest in all its different multiplicities in blood. The hunter who killed an animal would drink the blood of the animal, because in drinking the blood he became the vibration of the principal idea of that animal. It is a communion with the soul of the animal. Then the deer is you, or the lion is you. At some level, originally, when people ate meat, they didn't eat because they were hungry, or because they wanted to become carnivorous. They ate the meat because that is how they could connect with a principal idea or vibration, an archetype, as they were divinely guided.

Scientists tell us we have a reptilian brain and a mammalian brain within our human brain. Whenever these ancients ate food from these different forms—the birds or reptiles—it was because we have aspects in common. When they ate the meat, they were eating themselves. They were connecting with those parts of themselves. Whenever we eat a plant, in the process of digesting that plant, we receive certain forms of illumination. So I think the diet has to do with purpose. Because the ancient ones ate animals, we don't have to.

If you want to be a visionary, you should eat the meat of

a lion, either actually or symbolically. If you want to be a person who has a direct line, to be able to correctly define the metaphors that depict wisdom, you might want to drink deer blood.

We take into our bodies the things that feed the soul. We take in a vibration. Unless we eat knowing that we are taking in a vibration, we get stuck in the form, without realizing that we are not form. While we can recognize a form and give it a place, we need also to honor the idea that we are non-form, because beyond the form is another form, a more eternal, spiritual form.

I think of the Christian communion in which Christians symbolically drink the blood and eat the body of Christ. Bread comes from the wheat, a plant. When you are eating the body of Christ, you are taking on "Christ-like" qualities. The bread is the closest thing we can find to connect with the reasons that the Self is being and doing what we are being and doing at this time. It is a way to get in touch with the path, or rather, to become the path itself, the path that is resonating right out of the infinite self. That is what "bread-ness" means. Bread is the light of beauty, which is what Christ was. When we eat the bread of Mother Earth in holy ceremony, we are giving respect.

The main thing that ceremony teaches is respect. It teaches respect for oneself, for tradition, for other people, other people's traditions and ways, for the enhancement of life.

Judgment ≈ If someone is doing something that I don't think is right, the first thing I question is what role are they playing at this time on the planet. What is their real role, and is this what they are supposed to be doing? I ask those questions, rather than going on into judgment, because when I go into judgment, I know I am calling judgment onto myself. Judgment tends to block the divine process of life, not only for yourself, but also for others. So you don't want to judge too much because you end up with other people judging you. You create more of that kind of energy. Then you pick up judgment because that thought you put out is still around you. You create a hindrance for your own process through judgment.

Ceremony teaches us that everything that comes around goes around and that what we create is empowered by us to go around the circle of life. Eventually it comes back. It may come back in two or three seconds or two or three weeks, but it eventually comes back. Everything that we give returns to us, and that is the whole idea of the reflective universe. That is metaphor alongside our experiences.

In the beginning, everything was unity, but now we are living in the time of diversity. For this reason, we need to be careful about what thoughts we have, because as soon as we have them they are going out, and eventually they are going to come back. If our thoughts are positive, we are going to get positive stuff back, and if our thoughts are negative, we get negative coming back.

So, rightful living is important, because we are creating now what we are going to live tomorrow. Ceremonies of the living spirit teach us respect for that line of thinking.

It is all right for people to be where they are because that is how far they have gotten from where they started. Sometimes they actually have achieved even more than we have because they are coming from a place further along the line. Except that it doesn't always look that way to us.

Someone who is alcoholic or homeless actually may be a hundred thousand years ahead on his karma for doing that. He is suffering the cold out there, probably with no food, and maybe his liver is going out because he drank too much. All this suffering may be moving him further along karmically then we are. Who are we to judge what is going on with him, except that if we judge him, then at some point we are creating an energy that will judge us. That judgment means that when you judge somebody and it comes back, it makes it more difficult for your process; that judgment gets in the way. It is not even someone judging you now, it is just an energy.

Carrying and letting go ≈ Through ceremony there is a way of not carrying fatigue or problems from day to day. Through ceremony you deal with the problems so they don't usurp your energy, and the next day you start new.

The key to this discipline, this ceremony, is in a Tiwa word. *Tsclo-ii-eh* means "one is at rest." It is the combination of three energies, descending light, childlike innocence, and awareness. That is what heals you from tiredness. So your ceremony should combine these three energies: descending light, childlike innocence, and awareness.

One of the physical manifestations for awareness is water, so to increase awareness you might take a shower or a bath. As you are doing that, you just let go of today's worries. But it is not just a bath. For it to work as ceremony, the intention has to be there.

You could say the word *"tsclo-ii."*

Tsclo means rain that is falling on a parched landscape. When the rain falls it gives new light. That is the metaphor. That is the descending light, but it is the feminine because it is birthing, it is ever-growing. It is nurturing; it is a nurturing waterfall, nurturing rain. You say, *"tah tsclo-ii-eh." Tah* is "I am," so *"tah tsclo-ii-eh"* means "I am the one that is in a state of nurturing—a state of awareness, a state of innocence, a state of descending light."

Doing this ceremony will free you of the problems of yesterday without causing you to lose the thread of what you were doing. Anything manifesting in your life is an energy so strong it won't let you forget it. But when it does come to you the following day you're in a different continuum, so it is in a different layer. It is not impinging on your life any more, and you deal with it from an impersonal plane.

inspiration

This is the ceremony for renewal: get in the bath or shower and meditate on falling rain and on nurturance. Just let everything wash, because you're transforming yourself into a new being, into a new seed, into a new resonance. And then once you do it, don't second-guess it. Of course the mind will say, "Did I do it right? Did I do it long enough? Did I do it to the depths that I should?" Don't worry about anything. Just do it, and then go to bed. After doing it for three or four nights (or three or four weeks at the most), then the body just knows to do it.

Sometimes people will ask me about things we were discussing together three or four weeks before, and I don't remember what they are talking about. That is because, when I give a thing energy, at that moment I give it all the energy, all the focus, that needs to go into it. Today is a new day. Tomorrow I may not feel about today's concerns the way I did today because tomorrow is another day. I gave it all the attention it needed today and so tomorrow I will focus on something else.

Being able to let is go is important when I am working as a healer. The way I do it is to listen to the Tiwa word *kaa who*. *Kaa* means to heal; *who* means the presence of God. *Kaa* means something that is buried within. That is what I am healing or stimulating to be healed. That person has something buried that needs to be healed.

Kaa who. The very word tells you that when you're going to work with someone as a healer you're working with the inner resources or the inner self. When you work as a healer, you also know that you are not doing the healing yourself. You are just half of the process. The other half is God. God is the one that is going to carry it through. Therefore, you don't end up holding or carrying the illness. If you end up getting sick, that means that you are not totally in alignment with the power that is coming from the Great Spirit. Early on, good healers realize that they are not the ones that are doing the healing, but they're assisting. When I work with people as a healer. I just let the healing energy go through me, and I don't hold onto it.

Looking at patterns ≈ We came out of ceremony. All of life came out of ceremony. When a person is sitting alone on a room, that is a ceremony. In groups or whole tribes, people

From
the spirit
world
comes
Eagle
Wing to
heal the
people

inspiration

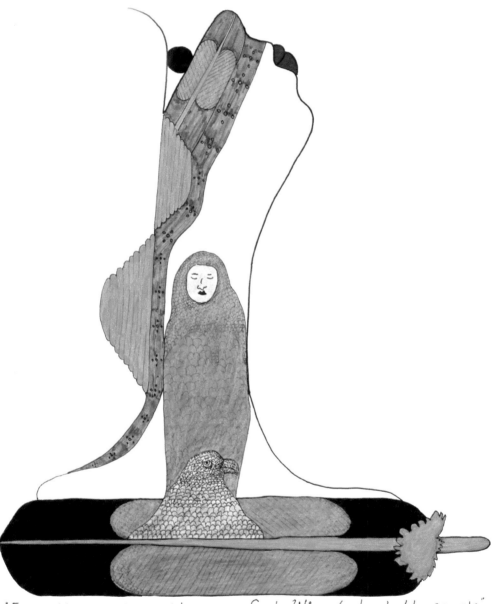

"From the spirit world comes Eagle Wing to heal the people"

once connected to ceremony by doing bear dances or grass dances. I know this may sound foolish, but today an individual in a building might do a window dance, or a book dance, or a lamp dance, or a desk dance, or a telephone dance. He can have a vision about that, or maybe you have the vision for people who can't have a vision right away.

Maybe your hands hold stones, and that would be the ceremony for the filing cabinet. And so you do that ceremony. You can access the metaphor. Find the archetype—the "great filing cabinet in the sky."

Here is how you might have a vision for a "telephone dance":

How many vowels are there in telephone? You have the "eh" and the "oh" sounds, so you start making those sounds, those vibrations. You stop eating—no food, no water—and you sit in the room, and you start chanting that sound, repeating that sound, eh-eh-oh. Maybe you do it five hundred times, chanting it slowly, or you might do it quickly in two minutes until you have a vision or you have an impulse of a ceremony to do. Then you do the ceremony. You don't do it for any other reason then to move yourself into the expanded reality where love and fear bond and become infinite knowing.

josephrael.org/
singtobowl.mp3

The chant to the telephone would be "Eh, eh, oh. Eh, eh, oh." It is saying placement, placement, childlike innocence in which the self connects to other beings. Write the word telephone: t-e-l-e-p-h-o-n-e

inspiration

Study the word. What does the "t" suggest? The "t" tells us that one of the things that the telephone is doing for us here is trying to help us achieve an even higher potential than we are achieving now. When God created the telephone—when

160

one day through technology we would have a phone—one of the reasons it was created was that it would push us to want to achieve a higher purpose.

When I do the telephone dance, one of the things I will look for during the ceremony is a corridor in which I can go beyond what

I am doing right now as a human being to something more. Higher potential becomes a motion. God is breath, matter, and movement.

Look at the next sound. The "eh" has to do with placement, so you write "placement." Now the "l" is a vertical line that makes a connection to all of the heavenly planes. What I see in this word is a grid, and the energy is coming into the grid down this vertical line. It shows that we have something pushing us toward our highest psychic potential.

Notice that placement is followed by the letter p, which signifies heart. So the phone it trying to find us a heart. The letter h has to do with everywhere-ness. If consciousness were a whole bunch of dots, h connects us with all those little dots, all reality. H is universality. O has to do with innocence, playfulness, childlikeness. N is the self. Notice that it is connected with innocence of the self.

Also, within telephone is the word one. Look for patterns in the word telephone. You see one, then there is the n and the e again, which is, again, placement.

So, having understood all those things, you review them for two or three minutes: placement, heart, universality, childlike innocence, self. Review those, but try not to think about them. Just repeat "eh-eh-oh-eh."

You are repeating the sounds now, and at some point when you least expect it, an image appears in your consciousness. An image will come. The image may be the motion you are supposed to make, or a new word. Then you chant this new word you've been given. You keep chanting. It is a process of elimination. The mind is very resistant, but at some point your body will start to move. You get the dance. You have to forget your body consciously and you get to the point where you know the body is there, but you are not controlling it. At some point, you will intuitively know the step. But you have to trust it and in the beginning you won't. Keep at it until you break through

and the body takes over. You are standing and then you chant,
you close your eyes, you begin to sway, you allow your body to
move in the chanting. You might begin stepping around, moving
your arms. Then you practice it, write it down. Then the next
time you want to dance to the telephone, including the spiritual
realm, you do the same dance.

Teach your mind to look at patterns. You go all the way back to the thing that holds the memory. That is the pattern of everything. Original ceremony is a living thing. It is alive in our gene pool. Actually, we are doing ceremony constantly, in spite of ourselves. When an office worker walks up to a filing cabinet and pulls out a drawer and reaches in and pulls out a file, and then puts it back, that is a ceremony because the office worker is moving forward, moving back. When you are sitting down, that is a holy posture; when you walk out the door that is a holy posture. The door itself is a holy posture, a metaphor. I think secretaries are blessed because they file and use computers.

Can you imagine all kinds of people doing a dance about a filing cabinet? Yet every object, every form carries a principal idea. All these forms that are around us are simply us, things that look strangely different, images that come out of the archetype of the living spirit. Ceremony itself is a living spirit. We talk about breaking our rigidly controlled concepts, which don't actually exist, but we find that when we use ceremony, it opens the principal idea behind everything around us. That is what the Christian missionaries didn't understand when they came to us four hundred years ago. They said, "You are dancing to a tree! That is the silliest thing you can do. You are worshipping everything but God. God wants a church." To them, dancing to a tree was pagan.

What the prehistoric peoples were trying to do was go through that doorway to get to the Source. We need ceremony to nurture us, but what we really need to know is how our lives are ceremonious. In that way, we understand that we are being nurtured. Yet, in order to understand, we still have to do the dance.

You do the dance for the filing cabinet, which was originally a big clay jar with scroll in it. You have the vision for the ceremony and then you do it. You are not really dancing for the filing cabinet or for the clay jar, but for the principal idea.

Dance means expansion ≈ When you walk up to the filing cabinet and open it, read something, put it back in and shut the drawer, that is also a ceremony, but not a formal ceremony. Dance means expansion. The reason for doing the ceremony is to expand the principal idea. You can dance to expand anything. If you want to know more about what a pen is, you dance it to find out. What is the door in terms of metaphor? If you can create a door dance, then eventually you can find out why buildings have doors. (I promise you that it is not just to have an opening to the room, nor just to shut out whatever is outside the building.) Knowledge, wisdom, and insight come from the expansion.

You want to start with what you already have. Start with chanting. Chanting brings everything into the here and now. It opens like a door and you can see through. You have to sing to the telephone or filing cabinet, to make the ceremony. Sing to the bowl. Sing to a deer that has been shot by the hunter. Sing to all of the different parts. The horns, the skin, the inner organs are open, full of ideas.

Let me go back to the world culture and the reason we have the telephone, or tape recorders, or desks, or lamps. We think we have them because it makes things easier for us, but I think if we really understood it from the place of metaphor, we would understand that these things are God talking to us. We can discover where we are spiritually in terms of the things that we use to make our daily living. They will help us discover our own imagery. They make up our life ritual.

Life was created, and all of the different physical forms, or mental forms, or emotional forms are created in our search for our beauty. Beauty is the only thing that is real. Everything else we do, we are doing in order to find beauty in ourselves.

One of the ways we find beauty is through ceremony. We have gotten away from ceremony because we went too far toward the rational side. The rational mind says: "Oh, that is not real, not important; it is ridiculous." Or, "I don't need ceremony because I understand what is behind ceremony." But something very important happens when we dance that form. It brings the form into the body as beauty and awakens in the gene pool the knowledge of the principal idea that created the desk or the lamp. The body is a part of our knowing. In the process of dancing (the motion or movement) we become the divine breath, creating new ideas for us to live by.

We need ceremony because our souls are dying of thirst. Remember, dancing is expansion. Expansion is moving us from the thing that is imprisoning us. We are breaking free.

Expansion increases our capacity for breath. Since we come out of breath, not out of movement, we have to go back to breath. Breath has to do with expansion.

The Unexpected ≈ So, we receive the ceremony and have definite instructions: we know the first step, the kind of singing, the kind of chanting, the duration, how often we are supposed to do the ceremony, the time of year it should be done, or if it should be done in the morning or the afternoon. Then, once the ceremony is set, at some point, we get an intuitive sense that we have to make a change in the ceremony that will make it slightly different than the original design we got. That is the unexpected.

Now here is what is important about the unexpected: When we have been doing the dance in a particular way for the last three times and all of a sudden we get this intuition that we need to do it differently, what is really happened is that a crack has opened from the infinite vastness and a gift has come through our ceremony to the planet and to the whole cosmic consciousness. We get an unexpected insight; we will feel it as a jolt; it will shake us. Now that is the real stuff, coming directly from our Maker. It hits us. That is the unexpected. The reason it does this is because that is the only way it knows to impress us with some new input, to come and touch us. Most of us go through life asleep, thinking that we are awake.

Otherwise there are guides, or gatekeepers in the four directions, keeping information out so that everything can stay the same. They are mental, emotional, spiritual, physical gatekeepers. Energy is coming in and going out. Gatekeepers won't let anything new in unless we can slip it past the gate. Ceremony is one way to slip things past gatekeepers. The unexpected is when we have the basic idea of how things are going to go for us that day, but on the way to the car, the unexpected happens, and we fall down.

Let's really study this momentarily. We slip and fall, and we weren't expecting to fall. At the moment, when we begin to fall and we wish we could do something about it but we can't, that is the only point where we are truly in a place of total and complete detachment.

Maybe the cosmos was created because God was walking down the steps and He slipped and fell. When He slipped, this reality was created between the time He started to fall and when He hit the ground. Maybe we were made from an accident; we kind of slipped between the cracks.

When the unexpected happens, that is when something new can come in. The necessary unexpected is what brings about evolution. I believe this very deeply. In fact, I live my life always praying for the unexpected, because the unexpected always brings wonderful gifts that I never thought could happen. I guess I get set in my ways, rigid about how I think things should be. The unexpected re-charges my energy as it gives me a whole new idea about the way things really are.

Puns and Metaphors ≈ "Who is God?" the student asks. And the Sufi answers, "Yes."

The Sufi has answered in metaphor, in a pun, because "*Hu*" means *God* in the language of the Sufi.

Puns, metaphors, parables, and stories are the teaching tools of the spiritual teacher in every tradition, including mine. Metaphors connect the world around us with the metaphysical, giving us a window on the infinite.

A metaphor is not simply a figure of speech. Metaphor is how God is present in our lives. We think in godly ways because metaphor is energy that is in a state of action, breathing life into ceremony.

Ceremony is how we, "the people" (vibration) cry for a vision. The souls of the people are drinking the sounds, 'ahh, eh, ii, ohh, uu,' the vowel sounds that occur in all languages. At the same time God (Higher Power) is providing the living inspiration (breath) of life to that process.

God is in everything. As we work with metaphor we discover the connections among all things; we enter the No-mind, God's mind. We become poets and artists, composers, seeing everything through the poetic, artistic, musical mind. We see things from metaphor and are filled with awe. At that moment we are coming from a base of love rather than a base of fear, because fear is an attribute of the rational thinking mind. Through metaphor we can go beyond the rational, to enter the all-loving, all-pervading mind of God.

Our rational, thinking mind does not disappear. It is fused with the metaphoric mind, the mind of God. In the metaphoric mind, there is righteousness based in love. The metaphoric mind swallows up the fear-based thinking mind.

Now, our souls no longer hunger for peace and solitude because at every moment the soul is being fed from this place of love. No longer are we stuck on the surface of the material, but we have gone through the material to reach its essence. Our souls are drinking the light of the essence of the material plane. The loving mind of God has swallowed the thinking

mind, owned it and swallowed it into the larger mind. At that moment all there is is love.

Everything that is perceivable to us is now showing us how God is kissing all forms into life, through breath, matter, and movement. God gives sustenance to life.

In other words, metaphor is how God insists upon inspiring

our innate God-given gifts—gifts we received at birth—into fully awakened states so that we may materialize them throughout our living moments.

In order to become people full of awe for life, we enter, through metaphor, into ceremonies of the living spirit.

The Dreams of Right Hand

joseph rael's visionary art

call my drawings and paintings "generators of light." When you encounter a piece of my art you're encountering a generator of a particular principle. For someone who has an understanding about sound, everything in one of my art pieces is a principle vibration.

In my painting with a hand and trees and houses, for instance, we have the power to manifest greatness then to allow it to exist for an instant and then to shatter.

As soon as I say "hand," I have a realization of what it means to manifest, because the sound for "hand" in the Tiwa Language of the Land is also the sound for "to manifest." Vibrations also work on the visual level; any time you see a hand in my art, it will awaken in you the power to manifest. I tell people to go down, down, down to the place where the archetype of hand-ness exists.

When we look at trees we know what greatness is — the vibration or energy of greatness. Houses mean "to shatter." The faces mean "to enter." Together faces, trees, and houses in a painting give us the power to enter into greatness and to shatter it. The feather means to give existence to the manifestation of greatness, to shatter it and to enter it. The lips mean "to grasp light." The darkness means to seek that which is not yet knowable. The eagle is *chee wah neh. Chee* is movement, beauty, awareness. *Wah* means the unexpected in this moment. When you connect it with all these other combinations, you have a window into a moment of the mystery of life. Like the different notes in a chord on a piano or a thousand violins playing in harmony, the elements in the painting work together to create a new vibration, a new song.

The
Dreams
of
Right
Hand

169

Everything is music, and it is playing all the time. What we need to do is get into the sound and flow of that music. Each of us is also singing for the rest of everything. Each individual has a certain music in each moment.

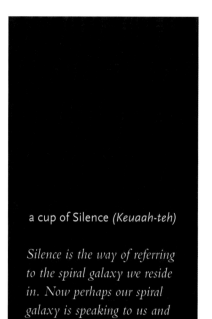

a cup of Silence *(Keuaah-teh)*

Silence is the way of referring to the spiral galaxy we reside in. Now perhaps our spiral galaxy is speaking to us and no longer sits in silence, and we, as listeners, will hear her call intuitively.

I could listen to music not only of my paintings but also of what I see out the window or in the room around me. The combination of all that I see would give me a vibratory resonance.

The reason I teach about the mystery of life this way is because on our planet we don't have that understanding

f Silence (Kevaah-teh)

anymore. The holy places are not just the churches and
synagogues and temples. Holiness is everywhere. Any moment
is holy. If we go back to that teaching we begin to understand
the sacredness of the beginning of life and we reacquire the
abilities that we had originally.

Ocean Place

Oceanus

Grea

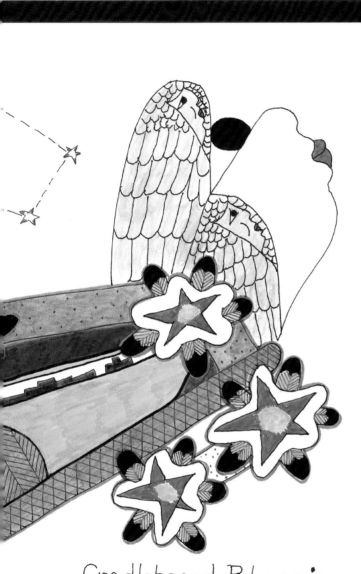

Cradleboard Blessing

r is the Big Dipper and the seven stars

© 2008 Ben title(
Beautiful
Arrow

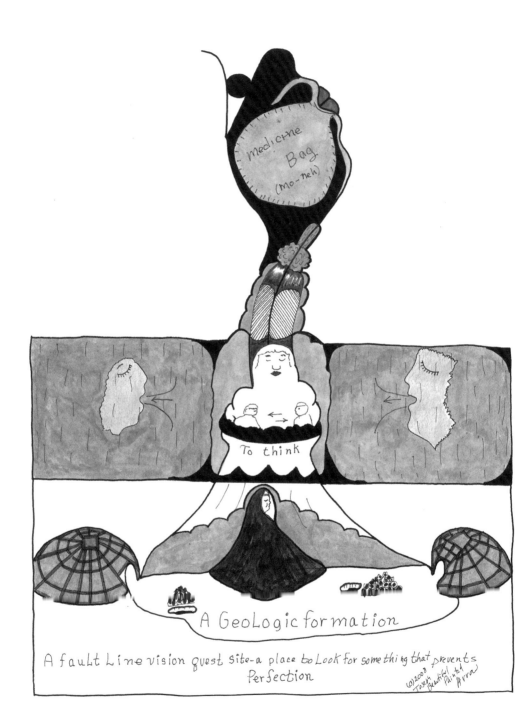

way of inspiration

The Earth is our Mother, and through her breath she gives us life and nurtures us with her insights. She inspires us beyond our own self-imposed limitations.

The Indians say this Earth is our mother and we are her children. In the indigenous language of the land that I learned growing up, we say the Earth is our *Gah-Teh-Meh-Nay*, our mother-father. Not father-mother, but mother first, and father afterwards. It is important to get this right. The mother-father principle is everything material, including both the Earth and the sky. It is the All-That-Is.

The mother-father principle says that we spend our entire life nursing. We spend our entire life suckling from the mother. By clothing us, feeding us, housing us, giving us breath, life, our livelihood, for ourselves, our children, our grandchildren, the Earth gives us everything we need. Life comes from our *Gah-Teh-Meh-Nay*, from our mother, our father, and we give back in return.

Something is leaving and something is coming in that has to do with nurturance, not just on the physical level. That coming-in and going-out is the Breath of Life. And it connects everything we are doing at this time at the cosmic level, at the planetary level. It operates at the individual level and at whatever task level that we are involved in at this time on the planet.

When anything is occurring, in any moment in time, it is occurring not only to the individual, but it is also occurring to that geography—to that physical geography. What is happening to me is also happening to this place, this continent, this Planet Earth, this galaxy. I am giving and I am receiving energy back from the Earth, and so are we all. We are receiving it, each according to what he needs and translating

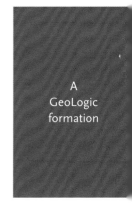

A
GeoLogic
formation

the energies we are receiving according to what we think is happening right now.

At the center of our spiral galaxy is a black hole. It is from this black hole in our galaxy that we are given mental, emotional, physical and spiritual consciousness. All two-leggeds are little medicine wheels walking around giving and receiving constantly from birth to death.

We are the seeds. We are the manifesters. We are the presence of God. We are the reverence. We are the blessed ones. We are the sacred, we are the holy ones. We are everything.

An understanding of principle vibrations behind inspiration gives a context in which to explain the supernatural. Here we deal with mystical knowledge. Mysticism is not the same thing as intellectual discourse, reasoning, or knowledge as one might study it at a university. Mysticism works on the level of intuition, of spirit. Some mystics say that the cosmos was created by numbers, letters, and words (sounds). Letters have to do with the materialization of ten vibrations via manifestation. This teaching is about the ten vibrations themselves. They are the one-to-ten of inspiration.

Remember that the cosmos is made up of five principal sounds, the five vowel sounds of "aah," "eh," "iii," "ohh," and "uu." In Tiwa, the language of the land, the words for the numbers one through ten contain these five vowel sounds. The Tiwa words for one through ten are:

1 = weh–mu

2 = weh–seh

3 = pah–chu

4 = wiii

5 = pah–nu

6 = mah–tschlay

7 = cho–oh

8 = wheh–leh

9 = whiii

10 = tehn–ku–teh

There is a Divine Presence in all the numbers. By listening to the vowel sounds in these ten numbers, we can access their powers. The sounds in the words for one through ten can teach us the ten steps by which material forms manifest from inspiration, the path by which the energy moves through all of perceptual reality into form. These are ten vibrations, ten seeds, ten stages inside the circle of manifestation, of all that is.

We are caught in this dimension of black light and white light, of breathing out and breathing in, of pushing away and pulling in, of avoidance versus embracement. Embracement deals with honesty. In embracement we have to be honest, we have to follow some form of moral law, moral tradition. In avoidance, we avoid work and try to go for comfort—but there is a tradeoff.

Living as we do in a world of duality, or what I call perceptual reality, we are thinkers, we are contemplators, because we are reflecting. We reflect something on someone, and they reflect it back to us. Or, the light is being reflected on the wall and it is being reflected back to us. That is what makes us contemplators, not that we are smart or that we are biologically built in a certain way. Instead, we are biologically built in certain ways because we come from *weh-mu, weh-seh, pah-chu....*

In other words, we come from movement. It is in our nature to have movement. Without movement we would begin to decline, then decay. When we go into decadence, we are returning back to no-form.

Movement is what created the ten principles of perceptual reality. If it were not for numbers, we would not have movement; we would not have inspiration; we would not have manifestation.

We know there are ten steps in the process of manifestation — not eight or twelve — because the hand is the metaphor in flesh and bone for manifesting. On the two hands, we have ten fingers, and the finger embodies the power to manifest from seed.

I've been studying mysticism since I was eight or nine years old, just because I was curious. The mystic, whenever he uses hand movement, like a handshake, knows that he is bringing something into manifestation.

In order for something to manifest, there must first be a seed. The fingers help us to grasp that seed or direction. The hands communicate. They can bring things to us or push things away from us. They help us to lift up or pull down, embrace or not embrace. It takes both hands—all ten fingers— to complete the vibrations of manifestation, because we cannot have one hand clapping. We need the duality, the left and the right.

The people of the Earth are receiving the blessings of the Horn of Plenty while we the people give these blessings to Planet Earth through our good deeds for others.

If we humans are going to continue to evolve, we now need to understand the vastness of who we are. We need to understand the vastness so that we can become that vastness, so that we can portray it by how we live, and live from that place of high potential.

We have vast potential because we do not live as individuals alone. We live as aspects of the Higher Mind. In the numbers one through ten, we can see the way in which the Higher Mind is set up to interact with and complement the human brain.

The numbers one through ten reveal the process by which the Higher Mind seduces the human brain, puts it in states of ecstasy, thus inspiring it to creativity.

Morning meditation practice: "All my efforts today will be for divine presence for all life. Amen"

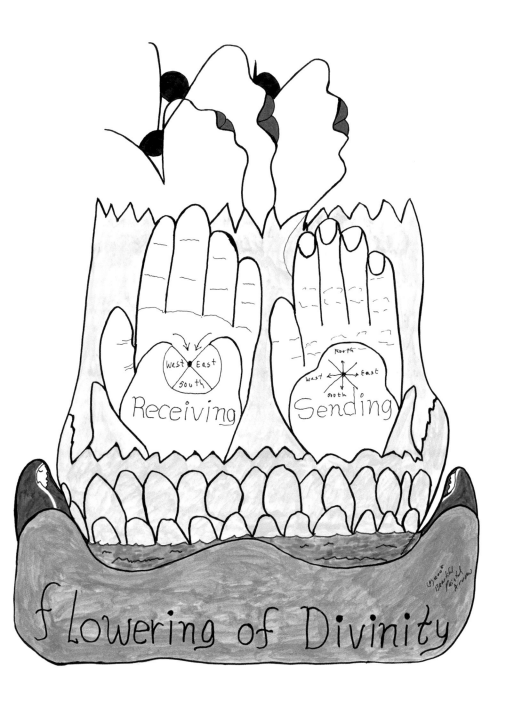

The Process of Inspiration ≈ The process of inspiration begins when the Higher Mind shoots an impulse of light and strikes a single nerve cell in the human brain. This is the first stage, the seed. This is *weh-mu*; this is the incoming form of meaning.

The impulse from the Higher Mind enters the human brain by way of the optic nerve neuron. Immediately the impulse produces *weh-seh*, known to mystics as divine longing. Now consciousness desires to create a form. *Weh-seh* is the point at which an intimate relationship is created between the Higher Mind and the human brain. We can now see ourselves doing a task. *Weh-seh* is stage two in the process of inspiration.

Pah-chu is stage three in the process, when consciousness gains the power of movement. Consciousness now has the potential to send out the form that it has perceived and desires to create.

Consciousness sends out the message to the rest of the brain. In step four, *wiii*, all the constituent parts of the brain receive or come forth to bring assistance to what is to be created in that instant of time.

At the fifth step, *pah-nu,* all the constituent parts of the entire human psyche (the self) come together into a oneness with the Higher Mind. That oneness is now set to take a given action. Now the person can grasp the idea.

At the step six, or *mah-tschlay*, all information or memory of past and present is reviewed. It is reviewed in order to glean whatever technical information is available that can be used for the creation to be constructed.

At stage seven, or *cho-oh*, all the constituent parts of the brain disappear into a devoted state of teachability and into that place between two slices of light.

At step eight, *wheh-leh*, the brain induces the movement toward the materialization of the form or forms, as it is now seeking a personal experience of it, a personal relationship with it.

At stage nine, *whiii*, a "yes" or "no" is given to the process, because the physical brain desires to know what compensation will be given for this action, if the action takes place.

At step ten, *tehn-ku-teh*, the physical brain either shelves the idea for later reference, or uses it toward a given act of creation.

Supernatural powers ≈ What this means is that we have powers beyond the physical realm. Inspiration is about the supernatural. It is not about natural powers or the logical discourse of the brain.

We have to give up all the early childhood socialization — the do is and don'ts —the assumptions about the nature of reality. Originally those ideas were put there as an opportunity for us to surpass them, to go beyond them. That is what parenting is about. It is to delude us, or to convince us to go off in a different direction. I think parenting is actually the best way of institutionalizing misguidance. I can say that because, technically, we don't exist.

But as we embrace the things we've been taught to avoid, we become the very dynamic of potentiality. We open up, and all of a sudden we have this awesome potentiality that we didn't have at fourteen, at sixteen, at twenty-five, at thirty-five, because the rules don't apply.

Someone said it a long time before me, and said it much better: "For those enlightened ones, rules, after awhile, cease to exist."

It is the same idea that Jesus taught — that the laws are put there, but once we really have the Kingdom of God in our hearts we don't need any laws, we just naturally act in the right way. It is like learning a new skill: first we have to practice according to rules, but once we get to a certain point, we can come out of spontaneity. We are empowered.

The rule is the radiance of light that has its highs and lows. The principle idea that created the original rule was formed by several component vibrations. The first one is that it has the power of radiance to have highs and to have lows. Ups and downs. The rule created carrying, the power to carry this radiance. We have highs and we have lows. The rule is a guardian of that and it carries. It has the power to carry the vibration of "as above, so below." That is the vertical plane versus the horizontal plane. The vertical plane holds the horizontal plane and gives placement to it.

And if the vertical gives placement to the horizontal, then inspiration can take form. So the rule asserts spiritual law, or natural law, because it locates the horizontal line in some particular place, whether high or low or in between, on the vertical line.

The vertical and the horizontal together form the cross, but the vertical is what rules it.

The vertical and horizontal also form the medicine wheel, the four directions. But that is only when we are trying to manifest something in a concrete way. Actually, there are no directions. There is no up or down or east or west, or north or south. We have the cross or the medicine wheel because these are ways of defining inspiration. These are ways of saying that the heart and mind have to become one.

The Esoteric Meaning (Powers) of One through Ten ≈ As we pronounce the Tiwa sounds for the numbers — *weh-mu, weh-seh, pah-chu, wiii, pah-nu, maah-tschlay, cho-oh, whiii, wheh-leh, tehn-ku-teh* — we are also accessing their powers of creation.

josephrael.org/ 1weh-mu.mp3

Remember that sound is powerful. Sound is actually the polarities coming together. One has to hit the other to make a sound. There has to be something hitting against something else, like two hands clapping.

In order to resonate the essence of these powers of creation, we pronounce the numbers in the language of the land.

Weh-mu — 1 — Slipping and Falling ≈ *Weh* is the principle vibration of the unexpected, of interruption. *Weh-mu* is the thing that comes out of nowhere. You're going along and suddenly you're interrupted and forced to change directions. Something has come from the realm of the unexpected that is going to effect whatever you're doing now.

Mu is "uuu," the essential vibration of carrying or potential.

The power of *weh-mu* is the first power to manifest; it carries with it the potential to create anything.

Weh-mu is the power of slipping from the one essence to

weh-seh (two), which is duality. The power of the One is the essential unity of diversity, and, therefore, inherent in the very nature of oneness is duality.

The reason we are sometimes unsuccessful in life, or we think we are, is because we avoid falling. We need to learn to fall graciously. We avoid falling, not realizing that if we would just allow ourselves to fall, we would harvest our highest potential.

Weh-seh — 2 — Hitting Bottom ≈ *Weh,* the unexpected, promotes higher consciousness because it forces us to do something we hadn't intended to do.

Seh is crying. We are crying for a vision. God is crying. God is actively involved in the creation of a manifestation. Whenever it rains, those are tears of joy from the Creator that make all things grow. Tears of joy irrigate the soul of the land. And what is soul? In Tiwa, the Langage of the Land, soul means "one who is drinking light."

Light comes from the heavens and so it is filled with the Spirit and is holy.

josephrael.org/
2weh-seh.mp3

It is in *weh-seh*, duality, that we have the power to cry. We understand longing, loss and tribulation. We understand separation from the One.

In falling we are passive, but in hitting the ground or the lowest place — when we hit bottom — we have acquired the power to manifest. Before then, we do not have it.

Falling energy is the feminine. The instant the energy hits, stops falling, it becomes the masculine. At that point it has physicality, mentality, emotionality and spirituality.

When energy hits bottom, it is placed. It stops, and this gives it placement. If the energy kept descending for all the eternities, then it would be nothing; no manifestation could happen.

When it hits, it becomes dual—two.

way
of
inspiration

185

Pah-chu — 3 — Movement in the Directions ≈ We go from *weh-mu*, to *weh-seh* (duality) to *pah-chu* (three), which is movement to all the directions of the medicine wheel. Now we have the power of movement. *Pah-chu* is the power to move as far as you want in any direction.

Behind every human power is the power of Divine Potential. Effort is sacred. *Pah* has the "aaah" sound, as in *tah-lah*, which in Tiwa means *work*. Work is worship.

We can also hear the name of Allah in the "aaah" sound, and *chu* has the sound of *Hu,* the Tiwa word for God.

Pah-chu, the word for three, means that all we have to do is show up and God works. God needs our physical bodies.

Wiii — 4 — Giving and Ascending ≈ In one, two and three we have done what we have done, and it has all happened at the center of the circle of light.

josephrael.org/
3pah-chu.mp3

josephrael.org/
4wiii.mp3

Now, with *wiii,* the powers of all the Directions come in to bring us their gifts.

We receive their gifts and, standing at the center of the circle of light, we receive the power of focus.

At number four, *wiii,* we have the power to give.

And, in giving, we have the power to climb, to ascend.

As soon as we give, we have ascended. That is why Indians always like give–aways. When we give, we ascend, we raise ourselves a rung on the stepladder, or several rungs, depending on how much we have given.

Wiii means that we give to life, life gives to us, and at that moment we have movement upward. The first thing we do, once we can move, is to give.

We have to give first in order to receive. For instance, if we are going to do a business deal, we have to give first. We have

to go into our dealings with the intent of giving. When we write a contract with someone, we have to give more to that person than we expect to get in the beginning, because it is in giving that we set up a relationship of exchange. When we give more, we get more in return.

This is one of the basic principles of manifestation.

Pah-nu — 5 — Crystallizing light ≈ *Pah* is the light of universal intelligence.

Nu is the vibration of carrying.

With *pah-nu* we are carrying the Vast Self of Light, the Infinite, the Eternal Light that never stops.

When you repeat an action, it becomes you.

Pah is light, universal light, universal intelligence. *Nu* is when that movement becomes something. It now has crystallized into a form. It has manifested. Now it looks like a plant, or a tree, or a two-legged. This is the first inkling that we have that it belongs to the resonance of "the people"; it has a vibration. Until the time of *pah-nu*, it can't vibrate like an apple tree, because it hasn't become an apple tree yet. Or it can't vibrate like a four-legged or like a two-legged. Form cannot occur until this moment.

Pah-nu is the stage at which energy takes a particular form. It is now identifiable. Like the seed sprouting and breaking through the Earth, it becomes a plant we can recognize. We are describing a process, a metaphor for the mysticism of how a moment germinates itself into existence.

Pah-nu. The thing is now identifiable.

josephrael.org/
5pah-nu.mp3

josephrael.org/
6mah-tschlay.mp3

Mah-tschlay — 6 — Bringing Forth Ancient Wisdom ≈ Once we have *pah-nu*, the next step is step six, *mah-tschlay*.

Mah means to manifest.

Tschlay is the vibration of ancient wisdom, lessons from the past.

What you do physically is supported by innate power of the land that is very old wisdom. It will facilitate a noble ending.

Ancient wisdom refers to spiritual laws. You cannot fail if you follow spiritual laws. If you follow spiritual laws in structuring a tribal government, it will go well for the tribe. The tribe is a spiritual entity. Then, every government has to be reorganized periodically, in order to bring that power back into perceptual reality. Every so often, the people have to ask, "Is that structure in compliance with our original objective?"

Mah-tschlay is to bring forth ancient wisdom. When a plant grows it is bringing forth its ancient form. A plum becomes a plum.

Tschlay means ancient. (It also means other things. It has multiple meanings.) So *mah-tschlay* is to bring ancient wisdom to the fore. Think about it this way. When we put someone on a job and that person begins to perform well, we say "He is beginning to blossom. She is beginning to blossom." The person is beginning to take hold of the task at hand. The individual can now make a contribution, according to his or her kind.

Cho-oh — 7 — Manifesting in Concrete Form ≈ Seven is *cho-oh*, when everything is at the stage of innocence.

Look where we are coming from — from six, *mah-tschlay*, bringing ancient wisdom from Source to the present. And then the next stage–seven, *cho-oh*–gives everything teachability.

Cho means everywhere. *Oh* is when everything is at the stage of innocence, in a state of teachability. *Cho-oh* gives everything teachability everywhere, on all levels: mental teachability, emotional teachability, physical teachability, spiritual teachability.

We have to concretize inspiration. We are concrete thinkers as well as abstract thinkers. Between the ages of eight and twelve we become abstract thinkers, but up until then we are concrete thinkers. Abstract thinking is the power we have to explain that which is concrete. We have to concretize the experience of life.

At step seven, the principle vibration of *cho-oh* makes it possible to manifest something in concrete form. This is the first time a concrete form is possible. It is not possible at step four or step five or step six. That is where the error is made, when people try to manifest something too early in the process. They don't take inspiration far enough to concretize it.

Wheh-leh — 8 — Expressing in the Circle of Life ≈ *Wheh-leh* — eight — is the moment at which the horizontal plane is created.

josephrael.org/
7cho-oh.mp3

way
of
inspiration

188

Remember that I said energy has to descend before it hits the ground. When it hits the ground, it becomes *wheh-leh*. In step two it has hit and come into duality, but it is still upright. It is not until eight that the energy begins to go horizontally. *Wheh-leh* means "It lies down." However, the energy is now moving at a higher level than when we began. We are exploring a whole new level of existence.

With *wheh-leh* we have the vibration, or power, to swallow, inhale, ingest concepts and give them life, give them breath.

Eight is the moment when inspiration has matured and now all those powers – *weh-mu, weh-seh, pah-chu, wiiii, pah-nu, mah-tschlay, cho-oh* – can be expressed. Earlier we got the powers; this step shows us how to use them. And we use them in the context of the circle of life which has east, west, north, and south continuing with energy going either sun-wise or moon-wise –going clockwise or counterclockwise. That means we can now think in linear terms versus non-linear.

When I was in graduate school in the late seventies, the theorists were saying that we learn abstract thinking at about the time we are eight. Long before then, by age three, we have acquired all the basic, fundamental forms we are going to be able to use for the rest of our lives.

Remember that the head doesn't mean thinking, it means focus — and the focus of life is spiritual— the spiritual path of the heart. We have to think through our hearts. We can't think through our heads. It is at eight that we have the power to think through our hearts.

Whiii — 9 ≈ With *whiii*, the number nine, the circle of universal intelligence brings the gifts. The seed is in the center of the circle, and now it is surrounded with the fruit. This is the harvest from the planting that also leaves you with seed for the next planting.

Circle is *huh-leh*, and it contains *huh*, which is seed.

Whiii means payback. It means giving. It is not exactly like the giving in number four. The number four is to give in order to ascend. The number nine is to give for what we have received.

josephrael.org/
8wheh-leh.mp3

josephrael.org/
9whiii.mp3

way
of
inspiration

Tehn ku teh — 10 — Completion ≈ Now we go to ten and ten is to stop. *Tehn-ku-teh. Teh* is completion, stopping. *Teh* is "amen." *Teh* means to stop. *Ku* means 'it is enough,' completion.. And that means the energy stops, because to stop is also holy. And we go back to the one.

Movement is holy, and to stop is also holy.

One-two-three-four-five-six-seven-eight-nine-ten. This process is going fast: Onetwothreefourfivesixseveneightnineten. In one moment, it has happened, but we have to go through all those seeds in perpetual reality. That is why life is so valuable here, because we have the powers of endowment that we have. We have *weh-mu, weh-seh, pah-chu, wiii, pah-nu, mah-tschlay, cho-oh, wheh-leh, whiii, tehn-ku-teh*, which we don't have if we are not life in a form.

The purpose of human beings is to manifest. That is why we come into material form. Through manifesting we push things upward. That is why we have hands.

josephrael.org/
10tehn-ku-teh.mp3

We are given life. We can't make life. We can't generate life. We can use life because we are manifesters, but first we have to receive it. Otherwise we can't make something out of it.

We have the power to destroy life, but we can't make it. I don't think we've gotten that straight; not at the really deep levels. We haven't really understood the reverence for life. We don't even know what reverence is. Too many things get in the way of a reverence for life: pride, jealousy, attachment, anger, mental obscuration (lying), greed, gluttony.... We have to remember that life is precious and we cannot create it.

We are not God. We are but God's echo: *iii-toh-che-loh*.

weh-mu — 1

The farmer is God planting.

The seed of life falls from the farmer's hand. It sails through the endlessness of space and lands in the furrow where it must lie until it germinates and divides into two parts, male and female.

One is the seed. The seed contains everything; all of the potential possibilities. *Weh-mu.* We inherently have all spiritual potential.

We need to understand our lives are really spiritual. Our wellbeing is spiritual. Through manifesting spiritually, we might acquire material things, but that is not the goal. The goal is a spiritual one, because "spiritual" defines itself as the

josephrael.org/
1weh-mu.mp3

191

power to inspire, or to be inspired. It is our reason for being. We don't exist just to acquire things in the material realm.

According to spiritual law, when we start off wanting to create something from a place of innocence, from a place that is not connected to greed, or jealousy, or attachment, or mental obscuration, or anger, but just from the fact that we have been inspired, then we are to manifest the fruits of our worth, of who we inherently are. And this will be the basis for the next inspiration.

If we haven't been inspired to do a thing, we shouldn't do it. We have to teach our children how to act from inspiration.

When we are inspired, there is a power that enters into our psyche that is not from this plane, that gives us not only physical energy but supports us mentally and emotionally. Power gives us direction and we become like madmen. Our whole life then becomes a direction, a statement of focus, a reason for being.

Inspiration is not contrived; it is not created psychologically. Systems that tell us how to create wealth don't work, because we want to do it mentally. Wealth doesn't come from a mental process.

In 1988, I had a vision. I was inspired to build peace chambers. Now there are peace chambers around the world. How did that happen? Did it happen because I had a lot of money and spent that money building peace chambers? No. It happened because when something is inspired, and we begin to talk about it, and it is God's will, it almost happens by itself.

We come out of potentiality, and potentiality expresses itself on this plane of perceptual reality through inspiration. And because we come from inspiration we have to be inspired in order to create. To be inspired means to have the Breath of Life give us life. Life — God — breathes life into us. And now we have spiritual bodies. The inspiration will come in on its own accord. All we have to do is let go of our blocks. We let go through movement.

I go to the Sun–Moon Dance, the long dances, or to the drum dances to let go of my blocks, because God is *Wah-Mah-*

Chi, breath, matter, and movement. If we are dancing, we are breathing. We are letting go of blocks and bringing in new physical, emotional, mental, and spiritual energies through that movement. Sundancers spend a weekend during the year doing the dance, and then for the rest of the 365 days after a particular dance, we'll have moments of inspiration.

What is it like for the dancer after the long dance, when we've danced through the night without stopping? After we get through our tiredness, there is a great clarity. We feel clearly placed in the world and happy. Then, we might have moments starting to break through every now and then, when everything seems to be shimmering and alive. Suddenly everything seems to be in connection.

But a person doesn't have to come to my dances. He can do this by himself at home. He can unplug the phones, close himself off in a room by himself for three days with no food or water, and just dance up and down; dance in place.

To be inspired is to allow ourselves to slip between two slices of light. As soon as it is cut through with a line, a moment of existence, then a potential thought has slipped between two slices of light. In that moment we have a thought. Each potential thought is a line slicing the light.

Receiving inspiration is not a matter of human will, it is an allowing. Native Americans have been practicing this for centuries, perhaps without knowing why it works.

There is a schism among Native Americans between those who want to teach the ancient secrets and those that don't. Those who really learn the ancient ways at depth come to understand that the ancient ways are not about keeping. The ancient ways are about giving.

But first we have to embrace the things we've been taught to avoid.

When we fall between two slices of light, we can consider ourselves as having been inspired to do something. Before that we haven't been inspired. We recognize that moment of inspiration because it stimulates us mentally, emotionally, physically, and spiritually. Inspiration is a physical stimulant.

In the instant an insight comes we are stimulated mentally, emotionally, physically, spiritually. The dancing, the chanting, and the fasting are ways to create the possibility of receiving inspiration.

The reason we need to do these things is that we tend to get crystallized, stuck in our patterns. We are used to walking into the house face first, so once in awhile we need to break that pattern and learn to walk into the house back first. Or, if we spent a lot of energy to keep from breaking our dishes, maybe we need to break one just in order to break that pattern. But be careful! If we enjoy breaking the dish we'll break a second one and a third one, and pretty soon we won't have anything to eat from. Instead of breaking a pattern, we set up a pattern of breaking dishes. We set up patterns because we have addictive personalities. Instead, we should be having fun. Life should be fun. Don't be afraid to break patterns.

Inspiration isn't planned. Inspiration isn't something that we do — step one, step two, step three — and we hope to be inspired. When we slip, we are not in control. We are forced to let go of control at that point. We have an almost instinctual fear of falling, so that is why falling is the very thing that we have to embrace. People who want to be inspirers or to be inspired have to first give up that desire to avoid falling. They have to be willing to fall.

Inspiration comes from the space of divine emptiness and manifests itself in the space of manifestation. Inspiration comes only when it can come forth into a realm of manifestations where there are no mental, emotional, spiritual, or physical presences. There has to be emptiness. Inspiration comes out of emptiness into emptiness and after it has come into emptiness, only then can manifestation grasp it.

Once something has been created, that is *nah*. It came via the path of inspiration, but now it is in a different realm. Once something comes into a state of creativity, from then on it is stuck in the realm of abstractness and concreteness — to its own peril, having left it up to the human condition to do whatever humanity is going to do with it.

In English, the word "one" sounds almost exactly like the word "want." To know what "one" is doing, you can say "one-ing … one-ing," and you hear "wanting … wanting." I sense that this is the point where sound creates divine longing in the world of illusion.

Inspiration wants to manifest. It is life that wants to give us something because it knows we can do something with it. We don't always know how or what to do with it. But it is up to us to see how we are going to use it and how we are going to manifest it. And that is when we get into the *weh-seh* — number two.

The word soul means "drinking light." It is like a cup, something that holds the substance. In Tiwa a cup is called *kola oh omo*, which means "beauty that defines itself to the deepest recesses of the infinite self, that carries with it power of teachability and has eyes to see." In other words, I am a cup. I am continually drinking the light. As I breathe and move and perceive and manifest, I am pouring from myself into myself. I am the drinker and the cup.

weh-mu
one

weh-seh — 2

josephrael.org/
2weh-seh.mp3

We cry for a vision.

The echo of Duality … divine longing.
It can now cry, and it can now come forth into the
Creation of Duality.

At step two we have duality, we have two sides, and at this point we have the capacity to cry. We can cry in longing. We can cry in praise. We have the power to cry because we have slipped.

Listen to it: *weh-mu* is one. *Weh-seh* is two. *Weh* is to slip. *Seh* is to cry. *Weh-seh* is to slip and see. We can now perceive.

We have slipped into perception, now we can cry, like when we cry for a vision.

Weh-seh is crying for a vision. And it is in number two that God has the plan for us that we are contemplators. We can think now, we can see, and we can reflect.

At this point we have a body. We have the right side and the left side of the body. We also have hot and cold. In the Tiwa culture at Picuris all the people are divided by hot and cold — the summer people and the winter people.

In terms of inspiration, when we get an idea, we ask ourselves the question, "How hot am I for it, or how cold am I to it? How close am I to success, or how far am I from it? These questions arise at step two.

We have to remember, however, that we don't have to analyze an idea to find out if it is an inspiration or not. We will know. What I'm discussing now is how that inspiration works.

This is one typology. Yet when inspiration actually comes to us, we can forget the typology. It doesn't matter.

I'm discussing how inspiration comes in ten steps, according to this form. Yet there are billions of forms. This is just one form. It is our form on this physical, material plane. This is the way *we* are doing it.

On this plane there are ten steps, and — *weh-mu, weh-seh, pah-chu, wiii, pah-nu, mah-tschlay, cho-oh, wheh-leh, whiii, tehn-ku-teh* — these are the sounds. But these forms are not for us to think about or to worry about, or to think we need to guide ourselves by. These are just forms by which inspiration is occurring in a split of a split of a second. We go from one to ten in less than a hundred-millionth of a second.

My Picuris grandfather and grandmother taught me that work is worship. That means we don't follow rules to become holy. Everything we are doing on the planet is holy. We simply move out of inspiration.

The Spirit of Inspiration doesn't leave it up to the human mind to think what it should be doing. Our instructions are given as part of the inspiration. We don't have to figure it out. If the complete picture doesn't come in the original impulse, then it isn't inspiration.

Inspiration is quick. It is clear. We might not understand all the details at first, but they are there from the beginning.

Our task is to live our lives in such a way that we have the highest potential for inspiration to come to us. We have to fall into a lifestyle that creates the possibility of inspiration. When we don't get inspiration, we get morbidity. We live in stress, anger, depression, and sickness. Yet these can also bring us back to inspiration. Sickness, for instance, forces us to break free of our self-imposed limitations.

Remember, everything we are doing on the planet is holy. Even if you were abused as a child, this is a gift. It brings you to *weh-ah*, to divine longing.

Step two is about that divine longing, for this is where we get separated from our Source. At step two we have judgment, and separation, and crying.

Even the parent who strikes the child creates a metaphor for inspiration. In the act of hitting is the vibration of *whah*. It is the form of light striking ignorance and giving it illumination. The parent is angry and sick, and he strikes the child, which is the form of childlike innocence. On some level he is trying to die back into a state of childlike innocence where inspiration can happen. And yet he is stuck in that form and that becomes a terrible pattern of behavior.

Whenever we get stuck in our patterns, inspiration cannot come through. We have to go on to *pah-chu*, to step three, to movement in multiple directions.

weh-seh
2

198

pah-chu — 3

josephrael.org/
3pah-chu.mp3

The farmer's hand — the Sower of Life

*The seed begins to root. It grows downward and to all the other
directions, for it carries the heart of life, of the clarity of all the
heavens. It now has a creation of songs and it sings its beauty. It
carries this beauty on its return to oneness of Maa-hay-nay.*

199

In step three, we have *pah-chu*, and we have movement.
Here we empower beauty to express itself. Beauty can express
itself because for the first time there is movement toward
completion.

Chu is carrying. In step three movement is carrying inspiration towards completion, and this movement, this completion, this carrying is beautiful. If we see it, we own it. If we own it, we move it. If we move it, it is essence, it is the seed, it is the food for our next inspiration.

If we see it, we stop it. In other words, we've grasped it. We have intellectual cognizance. We think we own it. Automatically, we move it. Movement creates perception.

Perception, by its very nature, is a state of impermanence. All of perceptual reality—this entire world that we perceive as material reality—is a state of impermanence. We keep trying to build things that will last forever, but we can't do it because we exist in this state of impermanence that is perceptual reality.

Remember, inspiration doesn't come from us. And because we are part of perceptual reality, we don't own it. That is why inspiration can't be given to us just once, forever. We have to keep our lives totally and continually involved in a chain of inspiration.

Our physical breathing is a metaphor for this. In fact, physical breathing is equated to inspiration. Inspiration is breath, my breath. My breath is my inspiration. In my breathing, there is potential for inspiration, because I've just breathed air into my body. Inspiration is not something that comes from some remote place. It is already an innate inheritance by virtue of the fact that I am breathing.

Now, when we breathe in, that is when we manifest. And when we breathe out, that is when we take notice of it. When we breathe in, we give it a name, an identity, a being. When we breathe out we give it sound, we give it physicality, we give it form. We put it in the context of mentality, of emotionality, of physicality, of spirituality. It is all in the breath.

Why do breathing exercises? Because it is in the inhalation that we are naming what it is that we are going to create, what we are inspired to do. And when we breathe out, we give it place, we give it reverence, we give it what it is going to be.

When we breathe out, we give it the placement of where it will sit in the constellation of beings, where it will be in relationship to itself, to everything else, to its state of being.

As for the manifesters who are trying to figure this out, we want to know why that is occurring. We want to have an intellectual sense of it. Yet, at the same time we realize that — so what? — we can't do anything about it anyway!

This is not so much a how-to teaching as a how-it-happens teaching. We are giving a voice to something that is already out there. We need that clarity. Without it, after a while we don't know who we are and then we spend a lot of time seeking for different forms that will help us to find ourselves and find ways of becoming inspired.

I have been teaching these things for many years, but they are just now beginning to have an impact, because people are now getting to that space where my writings have meaning for them. Ten or fifteen years have gone by now since I first wrote about the numbers in *Way of Inspiration*, and all of a sudden these ideas, these principles, are coming up more and more, as more people demand fuller knowingness.

> To promote health and prevent disease, simply repeat the ten steps, "Weh-mu, weh-seh, pah-chu, wiii, pah-nu, mah-tschlay, cho-oh, wheh-leh, whiii, tehn-ku-teh," as you are walking. When you are exercising, say "weh-mu, weh-seh, pah-chu . . ." and set up a cadence. As you do this, it becomes a part of your breathing. This path of inspiration then becomes your walking meditation.

pah-chu
3

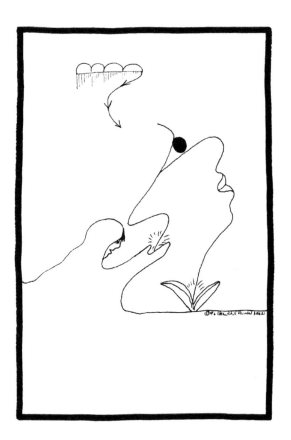

wiii — 4

josephrael.org/
4wiii.mp3

To give is to receive.

The seed of life begins to sprout and breaks the soil. Growing upwardly, it now gives. And so, the heavenly planes descend to give it a place in the Cosmos. Wiii is about giving.

We ascend at number four. From where we were, now we are going to climb up, ascend. Number four gives us that power to ascend, because we ascend in order to seek. We ascend in hopes of finding something even higher. We ascend so that once again we can fall.

Inspiration goes through a process of falling and moving us to ascend in two stages. We fall though one-two-three, ascend at four, and then go through five-six-seven, and at eight we fall again. At nine and ten we are ascending again, because nine is payback and ten is completion.

We have to give at four, but we give to go up to the next rung, realizing that when we go up to the next rung we are going to be seeking something new.

We give at step four in order to give ourselves permission to ascend.

These steps of inspiration are encoded in our experiences. All of the experiences that we are going to have while we are alive here on this plane are being given permission to reveal themselves.

I'm sitting down. Then I stand up, and my head is in a higher place. I have ascended. Maybe I have completed sitting down. Now I'm going to move on, and at some point, because I slipped into this reality via inspiration, I can slip down into my chair. Or I can slip down into my bed, or I can slip into another being. Slipping is an integral part of life at all levels because it originates out of inspiration, which is the original meaning of how life enters into the existence of physical form.

The pattern 1-2-3-4-5-6-7-8-9-10 is repeatedly appearing. Please understand that this is not something that happens only occasionally. This is a basic pattern in every experience of everything. Inspiration is the pattern of all experience, and the 1-2-3-4-5-6-7-8-9-10 is but an explanation of what that pattern is going to be. This is a movement that has been inspired and is either creating matter or de-creating it.

You see, technically, we don't exist, because matter is impermanent. Our skin is impermanent. Don't get stuck in the form, our grandparents used to tell us when we were children at Picuris Pueblo. Apparently, if we live from a place of reverence and respect and honor for ourselves and for life, we don't have anything to worry about because we are not attached to anything. We just do what we do because we do.

Because we are who we are, we are always going to be

statements of "looking-for," "searching-for," because searching for more knowledge, more understanding, is the same as ascension. We are innately seekers.

And look at the metaphor: Jesus ascends. This is the metaphor for breathing. We are breathing all the time, and in Tiwa the soul is defined as that aspect of life that is drinking the light of All-That-Is. So all of life is breathing. We can call it energy, we can call it biochemical interaction. But still it is the breathing aspect of the soul. So, if we know that is ongoing, then we are automatically endowed with the potential to be inspired at any moment. And anyone in his right mind ought to have enough sense to be open for those moments when inspiration enters. And anyone ought to be able to act upon inspiration, because that action on that moment of inspiration is how one exercises one's gift of potentiality.

Inspiration will come according to the direction that we have been inspired. But what that inspiration is going to look like is not known to us until it occurs. We were created as two-leggeds. If we were elephants, we couldn't get the same inspirations that a human might get. And if we did, we would take that inspiration and we would perceive it according to the way an elephant sees it, which might mean eating peanuts or plowing in the field or leaning against a tree. Likewise, a plum tree takes its inspiration and produces plums, while I might take inspiration and produce a picture or a song or a book. Other people take inspiration and start a business.

At first, we get a big inspiration, and then there will be smaller inspirations or insights that will follow. But the intent is in the first inspiration. In shamanism, we don't plan out the steps of the process. We just know what *weh-mu, weh-seh, pah-chu, wiii, pah-nu, mah-tschlay, cho-oh, wheh-leh, whiii, tehn-ku-teh* is. We honor those ten vibrations and we say, "Look, this is what I'm going to do." And this is what gets done.

Of course we live in the physical, material realm, so, it is okay to have a plan. But don't get stuck in the plan. This is what works for me. This is how I live from one inspiration to the next. This is how I stay in my potentiality. I'm not here to belittle the whole idea of planning. I worked for the University of New Mexico. I wrote some of their funds proposals, and they even got funded. I am a very practical man, and wherever I can save, either financially or otherwise, I do it. But I also know there is another power that also works with me and that power I have absolutely no control over. I don't control anything of what it is that other power is going to do. And yet, when it shows up, it is very clear, and I know it is God's presence.

This is what that realm *is*. There are a lot of books on planning. What I am suggesting here is, once we decide what we want to do, we can get rid of our plan. In the original inspiration, we are going to get everything we need to know. It is not the result of our planning. We are going to get to God in spite of ourselves. We can't get to God by thinking, but we don't have any better sense than to keep trying. It would be easier if we'd just leave thought out of it, but we are going to get to God in spite of our thinking. Once we get the goal, the inspiration, we can just forget the plan. If we are going to worry about the plan, then we are going to keep going back to God and saying, "No, I want to do it my way."

Inspiration wants to give; it wants to give at the point of four. It is important for us to give because that is what it takes for the spirit of inspiration to give to us in step four.

Inspiration comes from the up-above. Inspiration is an accumulation of all the potential possibility that comes through as breath when we inhale and exhale. Maybe scientifically breath is oxygen and carbon dioxide, but, actually, breath is a pattern of inspiration that exists already in our lungs. We have absolutely no reason to think about it. All we have to do is breathe.

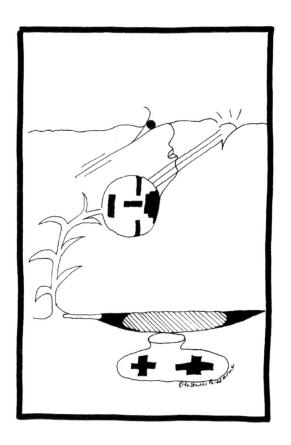

pah-nu — 5

Form

josephrael.org/
5pah-nu.mp3

*A stalk appears, moving toward the sun. The enlightenment of
the self gradually emerges and merges with the sky of the sun.*

Step five is *pah-nu*. At step five, energy, inspiration has taken
a form and is now identifiable.

In step five, the self — the infinite Self and the personal
self — glues itself to the power of carrying. And this is the
connection of the heart and the mind, when the light fuses
with the universal intelligence that connects infinity with the

personal self in the act of carrying. Now it knows how to carry inspiration. This comes at the point of five, not at four or at six. It knows this at five for the first time.

Actually, there are no steps. There is no one-to-ten process, really. All I'm doing here for our discourse is taking a flash of an instantaneity that occurs extremely fast and slowing the energy down so I can give it to you in linear perspective: 1-2-3-4-5-6-7-8-9-10. But actually it is just one flash of light. I've seen it. It is a blinding light that flashes on. It goes as far as the boundaries of the circle of light and disappears. And I disappear as part of that light. At that point of inspiration, everything disappears. It is all nothing. We are not there. We are everything, but nothing, simultaneously.

Linear time is what we do. We divide that rapidly moving light into increments of time by slowing it down. It is one movement, but it has ten aspects. We are trying to explain the supernatural. I guess we have to do that because otherwise we wouldn't have a mind. We are caught in the reflection and perceptual reality, and the way we perceive is by writing things and talking about them. We do this because we love it. We love it, because we are in love with life. What Tiwa thought tries to do is explain why certain things are occurring here by virtue of the qualities that make potential a possibility. It is trying to explain potential by talking about inspiration and how inspiration is occurring. Inspiration is the key to life. It opens up the door for manifestation.

We are carrying the five essential vibrations of God in each of our hands, because on each of our hands we have five fingers. Five is the power to manifest. Five is also the power to turn loose.

pah-nu
5

5 Rabbis

Several years ago I had a vision to capture the two War Gods whom pueblo creation stories say came from the underworld with the people, to help protect them.

In the vision I saw 5 rabbis in black robes and hats. I thought of them as the five fingers of the hand and also the 5 vowel sounds that carry the principal vibrations of the universe: "aaah," "eh," "iiii," "oh," and "uuu."

They were dressed in black because everything came from the black light. (My tradition doesn't believe that black is evil or black is a void. On the contrary, we believe black light is so pure that it can't be seen.) White light is made up of red, yellow, blue and all the vibrations of all the colors. Black is pure. Black is poh-neh-neh, and poh is blowing breath; neh neh is the self, positioned in awareness of the Vast Self. Black is the breath of life. Medicine people have always used breath to bless and heal people, because breath carries with it the black light of all potential, of all life.

The 5 rabbis were in different parts of the world, but they came together in my vision. They told me to go get the war gods and bring them home.

To be in a state of war is to be in puu-tie.

pah-nu
5

Puu is carrying. Tie is inside. Puu-tie is to make the qualities inside us manifest as outer qualities of our being. Whatever you are focused on gets carried out there. You verbalize it. You call names.

To send the war gods home, in effect, was to take away that vibration of puu-tie.

Since the war gods were sent home, we on Earth are no longer warlike. We are just warring out of habit, but our hearts aren't really in it.

mah-tschlay — 6

Corn

The plant grows outwardly and begins to bring forth its fruits.
It now knows to bring into wakefulness in itself that which
is ancient.

josephrael.org/
6mah-tschlay.mp3

Number six, maa-tschlay, says we are bringing ancient wisdom into the present. We now have the power of perceiving past, future, and present as an orientation.

Another way of saying it is that, beyond linear time, we are creating that which is ancient in the here and now. It just takes a different profile. It looks different than it did 100,000 years ago because we have evolved 100,000 years.

Everything is going to look different now, but it is still basically the same design, the design of inspiration. But now we are in a different place on the evolutionary chain because we are in this perceptual reality, which is a state of impermanence, always changing.

Step six, *mah-tschlay*, is basically about time, because it means to bring forth from the past, to bring forth from the ancient.

Mah means to bring into. And *tschlay* means old. So *mah-tschlay* means to bring the old into the present. At number six we have the power to determine what is past. Now we can relate to what is past. We honor our ancient lineage. We honor memory. We need to do this because we think we are here. We think we are in something called the present, and that this is the only time we can relate to. As soon as we place something, fix it in a place, we are probably in trouble.

We follow a particular design in order to achieve our highest potential. We are made of potentiality. We have to start with the idea that we *are* potential. We are the seed and every seed is a potential.

We take the seed for granted, but I don't think we really know what it is. We have no idea of our own potential. We have difficulty, because from our early childhood we are taught certain dos and don'ts, depending on the culture that we come from. Actually, we have inherited many, many more powers than we ever use. These powers come into play when we embrace the things we have been taught to fear. They are innate in us no matter what culture we come from. We have these powers by virtue of having been birthed as human beings.

A thing has to take form according to its nature. When we understand that, we will embrace all of our innate powers. We run into trouble when we avoid rather than embrace.

Suppose, when I was five or six years old, my mother said to me, "Don't play with matches, Joseph." But now that I'm 25, and somebody says, "Go light a fire, Joseph," I can't do it if I'm still afraid to play with matches.

I am thinking of inspiration as a light that enters into our psyches. And we are teachable, because light is teachable. It carries that power, the power to learn. We are not teachable by ourselves. By ourselves, we don't have any of these powers. By ourselves we are nothing.

I think someone said it better. They said, "By myself I am nothing, Lord God. Through You, I am."

I believe that inspiration is God's presence, which we here call life.

People tell me, "I want spiritual healing," or, "Spirit said for me to do this, Spirit said for me to do that." But nobody has taken the time out to tell me what Spirit is. Spirit is the power of inspiration. It is the presence of the breath.

The breath is God's presence, which in this case, and for us, is life.

Remember that we can't make life. We are pretty good at taking it away. I might take a houseplant out of its pot and kill it, because convenient to do so. I can dam up the river so I can irrigate the dry land. We stop the natural flow of things. We can't make life, but we can interrupt it. We don't understand what life is. We think we do, but we don't. And, as soon as we think we do, we are in trouble because thinking is not in the realm of inspiration. Thinking is in the realm of the unfolding of that inspiration in a very constricted place called materialization.

As soon as we start to think, we have crystallized the energy. It is not free anymore. We are doing ourselves in by the very nature of thinking.

Thinking isn't a bad thing; thinking is the same as illusion. Thinking is occurring within the realm of illusion. Pretty soon, because we live in the realm of illusion, we start believing it is true.

Take, for example, the houseplant, a geranium in a pot. The geranium has physical form. Since it is in a physical form, and since it is in a physical pot, after a while it is going to say in its genes, "The only place I can live is in a pot. That is my lot in life."

But that is not what that geranium is. That is just what it looks like at this time.

Appearance and perception are the same. The plant is perceiving what it is. But what it is perceiving is simply its latest form. It is perceiving its Johnny-come-lately state, a perception of the present moment.

By talking about the steps of inspiration, we can get beyond perceptual reality. We can begin to understand that we are so much more than our present state of being. We are God's potential. Unrestricted.

I'm not saying this on my own authority. This is the teaching from my Tiwa-speaking people. Tiwa is saying that we are endowed with limitlessness. We are priceless; we are eternal.

Seven says it. Seven, *cho-oh*, teachability, is saying that we have the power of awareness at all levels. Seven says that we are everywhere.

You see, our early childhood socialization taught us just to focus right here. But we are everywhere, right now, at this moment. We are consciously aware every moment of everything that is going on. We have accepted a skewed version of reality, so this is all we are seeing. We only see this version because we happen to be in these bodies here. Actually we have billions of eyes, everywhere, seeing, because seeing is movement and movement is what assists the materialization of what is perceptual.

Without perceptual reality, we don't have the materialization of a form by which matter can control and crystallize itself into placement so that there is radiance ... intelligence.

Here is what seven is like:

Think of the cosmos as one large room. It has the power of perceive-ability at every single inch – every single cubic inch of this room. But we only see a tiny little part.

Remember, we said we were using the sounds of the numbers to discern what was happening at each stage. Remember that we said the "oh" sounds means childlike

innocence or teachability. That is how we know that seven, *cho-oh*, has to do with teachability.

Remember, too, that it takes two hands for clapping. At first the energy is just one, and the number two splits it. As long as it is just one hand, we can't hear its vibration. So, it takes these two together. First there is unity and diversity. Then *weh-seh* causes polarity, and then three is reconciliation. From reconciliation, we go to number four, which is the purpose, which helps us to ascend. We are here to ascend. Number five, connects us to *thlon-nay*, which is the light connecting itself to infinity. Then we can carry. Then, *mah-tschlay,* ancient wisdom, can manifest.

None of our actions that have to do with purity, that have to do with awareness, that have to do with carrying, that have to do with innocence, or placement, are things that we are doing new this year or in this eternity. It all goes back to the beginning, before the cosmos was created. Perhaps over here it is manifesting as the action of driving a car down the road. The wheels are turning, the car is moving, it is being held on the road by gravity, and we have a lot of other things going on. If we need to know what is the essence of the event that is happening today, we perceive it as it was in the past. We can know what it manifested as billions and billions and billions and billions of years ago. It was inspiration then, and it is still inspiration. It is just that this is the way it is manifesting now.

When we say God is everywhere, that is the vibration of seven.

Teachability is when an idea crystallizes and places itself as a statement of awareness. It crystallizes itself into awareness in order to connect the infinite self to the personal self so that we can be a statement of goodness. That can't happen before seven.

The inspiration has to crystallize again so that awareness can fuse itself to the infinite vastness. The infinite vastness is not just this cosmos but the totality of all of the billions and billions of cosmoses. Now, for the first time, we have announced a statement of goodness in that teachability.

That is why we are attracted to teaching and to learning. We are not attracted to learning because we want to be smart. It is because learning is an innate process of cosmic consciousness. And that innateness has to do with how the cosmos is fused together in a gravitational attraction, or a cosmic resonance that brings itself into a cluster of knowing. That cluster of knowing is made up of crystallization, placement, clarity, awareness, self, and goodness.

Interestingly, goodness is an integral part of death, because in perceptual reality, we have life, death, and rebirth, so we are going to stop dying only when we give up trying to know. Until then, dying is a part of the road we follow, because inspiration apparently is what we are asking for: To know is to be eternally awake.

I've looked at this question for a long time because I've spent my life working on a shamanic level for peace. People ask me, "Well, what is peace? What is war? What is death?" I'm interested in knowing how the phenomenon occurs to start with that eventually ends up looking like death or war or peace billions of years later. What is the source? I don't think we can really talk about mysticism and leave that part out. If we are going to really deal with life, we have to understand what it is at the source. We need to know it and we need to bless it. We need to give it reverence.We need to understand life by exploring the power of teachability. Teachability is what is at the basis of evolution.

That is what we are saying, and that is what Jesus was saying. He could do anything we can do, including sin, but if we are going to live here, we have to understand life's parameters. That is the law, the Ten Commandments. Follow these and we are home free! He didn't put it quite that way, but

that is what I think.

Life puts us in a very interesting place, a holy place, a sacred place, where we have awesome potential. But we don't realize our potential. We avoid, deny, or suppress. And we are hesitant to embrace the things that we were taught to avoid.

To embrace something, we have to deal with honesty. And

we don't really want to, some of us. Why should we? We have free will. We are forever going off the deep end into some illusion. We can't judge others. For instance, I can't tell the car dealer next door to stop selling his Cadillacs. I don't even own part of the company. But it seems like that is what we try to do. Rather than wasting our energy on judgment, we can spend it on the things we can honestly do something about.

In a sense, goodness is when all the potential possibilities of the power of inspiration are unfolding as they are supposed to, and our job is to be in the dynamics of that process and not question...*not question*. Whatever we can use a rule on, we will because we can. But there are some things we can't force, and we need to be aware of what those are.

We cannot tell inspiration what to do. But once we get it, we can direct it according to the ways in which it has instructed us that it wanted to be used. Inspiration takes an awesome responsibility away from us because it is telling us what to do, what to be.

Because we need money to participate in the economy, in the socio-economic and political system that requires money, after a while, it is money that inspires us or pushes us to create. So we continue to create for economic reasons, rather than for spiritual reasons. But in the foundation, our impulse to create came out of inspiration rather than the motivation of materialization. Materialization is not bad, however. When something is inspired, that power that inspired us is going to make sure that we have success. That is its job; it is going to see that we are successful, if we follow what that inspiration tells us to do.

Success is not based on how smart we are, or what assets we shifted around or what great deals we made. Success comes when we follow inspiration, when we give ourselves to inspiration. Then inspiration will continue to give us the physical energy, the mental energy, to unfold that plan that it told us to do, and this will require very little effort on our part. It will bring to us whatever people we need to further inspire us.

If people really grasped this truth, it would break all of the precepts, the concepts that keep us in bondage. At some point humans are going to remember that we come from inspiration and that we continue to be inspired.

cho-oh
7

wheh-leh — 8

The horizontal dimension

Ears of corn have matured. The corn falls. It lies on the ground.

josephrael.org/
8wheh-leh.mp3

At the number eight, we have to fall.

Weh-mu is the circle. *Pah-chu* means that it is everywhere. *Wiii* means that it has the ability to go up. In eight, or *wheh-leh,* the horizontal dimension is added. At first we had the above and the below. Then we had a circle — the energy going sunwise and moonwise (clockwise and counterclockwise). Now, in number eight, the energy lies down.

At some point, everything has to lie down. When we are standing, we are in the vertical. As soon as we lie down at the end of the day, we become number eight. So we are "doing eight" every twenty-four hours. If we clock twenty-four hours as one day, then during that day, at some point, we have to lie down, because our physical body is built that way, and also because it is honoring *wheh-leh*. *Wheh-leh* is number eight, to fall. So, in fact, we lie down to rest because inspiration is also saying we have to fall into the foundation of life.

> The sheep is the symbol of foundation. When we put the hide of a sheep on anything and we sit on it, we are sitting on the foundation of life. When we do our sheep dance at the Picuris Pueblo it is to honor the foundation of life. The sheep is the metaphor, it is a symbol, it is the sacredness of foundations.

Wheh-leh is to fall. Remember I said that we need to do the things we are taught not to do. We have to embrace the very things we were taught to avoid. We were taught not to fall, to avoid falling. Now, at the point of *wheh-leh*, we must embrace the fall. Otherwise, we can't complete the creation. Inspiration is already telling us, "I will inspire you. But my inspiration will come to you without your having to do anything. It is just going to come as a gift to you."

Inspiration is a gift for us. We don't have to earn it; we don't have to work toward it through meditation or chanting. We don't have to do a sacrifice. It just comes.

And one of the qualities of inspiration is that it falls on the ground because apparently, we are stuck in gravitation, in the gravitational phenomenon of falling. As soon as we fall, we have masculinity, which means to unfold or embrace it. The masculinity, when we fall at number eight, tells us to honor it, to honor falling, to embrace it. Because then we let it go. We do this when we go to bed. We don't argue about it. We say, "I'm tired," and lie down. We fall asleep.

Look at the symbol for eight. It is the symbol of infinity when it is a lazy eight instead of an upright eight.

So far we've been dealing with energy that has been going up and down. Now, in *wheh-leh* it is going horizontally. The energy is now more physical and mental, whereas, before, it was spiritual. Now it has mental and physical empowerment.

In other words, when inspiration comes through me, at the number eight, I have received. I have now grasped. I now know. I can now move the power of that bonding of my physical body with my mental body, so that now I can carry on a discourse from that perception, from that standpoint, from that resonance, from that understanding, from that moment.

wheh-leh
8

whiii — 9

josephrael.org/
9whiii.mp3

Capacity to receive

The Ground (infinite) eats the corn. It dies into the cold
(movement), returns to the Creator of the winter season ... back
into the dream.

Step nine, *whiii*, has to do with payback. It is time to pay
back what we have been given.

It is a payback like that when we eat. Eating is a celebration
of that food that inspiration has created. At least, Indians think
of eating as a celebration. Celebration was created by beauty

that found a place in resonance, so that it could exist with the heavenly and earthly planes, so that it could create a movement of clarity and purity.

Eating has to do with digesting, transforming. We transform matter to energy. We pay inspiration back the energy it gave us.

Payback is an important step in taking the inspiration to its completion, to number ten.

The farmer out in the field waters the plants, works in his garden, and at some point he harvests the crops, brings them in, and he eats the fruit of his toil.

When we eat, God celebrates with us the gift of inspiration.

There is a Christian prayer that says, "Bless us O Lord, and these thy gifts which we are about to receive from thy bounty." What we are saying is, "Thank You for giving me the privilege and honor of being in Your Presence."

There is an enormous wealth here, the wealth of Presence. Now life is thanking life for life.

The mouth is *tschlah-moh*. *Tschlah* means "greatness," and *moh* means "to see." The power that originated mouthness before anybody had any clue what the mouth was, was greatness that fused itself, that glued itself, to the being of perception, so now perception can see. And, apparently, when we eat, we can see. In other words, if we didn't have greatness, the mouth-being would never have been created, and the mouth-being would never have had eyes to see, so that we would not have had perceptual reality.

The moral of the story is that everything is eating everything. We know we eat plants, and these plants are eating something, and that something is eating something else. So in this realm, we are eating ourselves. We know that every species of animal has a predator. Everything is eating everything because eating has to do with the mouth and seeing. The mouth is greatness, so eating is "seeing greatness." And since we are made of potential possibility, potential possibility has to do with trying to achieve our highest potential, and the only way we can achieve our highest potential is through seeing what we are being and what we are eating. The brain is eating what it is seeing by virtue of grasping it and digesting it as principles.

We might think about a bird of prey that swoops down and catches a mouse and eats it. As soon as the digestive enzymes of the hawk or the eagle start to digest the mouse, the mouse then, at that moment, has found its connection with God, because at that point of digestion after death, there is a moment of ecstasy, a celebration, for the mouse and for the hawk.

It happens because the hawk has a reptilian brain and the mouse has a mammalian brain, two of the three different brains that are fused in the brains we humans have. When the hawk eats the mouse there is an integration of mammalian brain into reptilian brain.

Integration and eating are synonymous. They are one in the same power.

> When a baby comes into this world, its first gesture is to suck, and the baby's suckling blesses us. This is because we have three brains, the reptilian brain, the mammalian brain, and the human brain. The human brain is the rational, frontal-lobe power that is not instinctual like the reptilian brain or like the mammalian brain. When we see a newborn baby that wants to suck, we are blessed on an instinctual level. Our mammalian brain is blessed.

Digestion means "to plant." When the reptilian brain and the mammalian brain are integrated in digestion, God then plants the next field of reverence, of resonance.

Digestion transforms the energy to what it is going to be next.

It is really very simple. We are who we are because of what inspiration is doing. Here is the design that automatically sets up a power to endow ourselves with cosmic knowing. Inspiration operates by natural laws. Inspiration doesn't have anybody to police it, to take care of it. Inspiration takes care of itself.

Yet we have many hospitals and a lot of illness on this planet. There is sadness and dysfunction. It has been said that eighty-one percent of the people come from some kind of dysfunctional family. We have tried to formulate inspiration and we got caught in using punishment and coercion. We tend to formulate ourselves right into a corner, then we complain because we are not happy with our self-imposed limitations. Maybe it is because we haven't understood our place.

We are not responsible for creating inspiration. If we look at inspiration, it tells us what we need to do. And if we follow it, there is nothing to think about. We have a choice about whether to follow inspiration or to think and formulate. That is what throws us off. We think and we get into trouble by thinking. But if we let that process unfold by just following its dictates, what it tells us to do, we get where we need to go.

Inspiration is going to tell us from A to Z what to do. Why not do it?

whiii
9

tehn-ku-teh — 10

It no longer exists as it was.

josephrael.org/
10tehn-ku-teh.mp3

It is no longer corn. It stops being. It freezes. It has become again the Essence of Breath, Matter and Movement, before Creation.

Last we go to number ten. Number ten is *tehn-ku-teh*.

Number ten says, "Enough is enough. That is it. Stop. It is over, let's go to one again."

This step is the one that puts the top on the vertical line, to make T.

Here it is again: There is total emptiness, nothing, just space. And then there is a spark of life that appears at the center of the circle of light and goes out. It goes as far as it is going to go and that is an instant. And it returns to the void.

And, again, a spark of light goes out, returns and another moment has occurred. Ten steps happened and an inspiration has transpired.

What does "transpire" mean? It has to be related to respiration, to inspiration. Breathing in and breathing out.

And that is it. Really, all I have to do is breathe. I can do a meditation of breathing if I want, or I can just breathe. Inspiration doesn't require me to do anything except breathe. So why have we studied inspiration? Because now we know how it is occurring, and we can relax.

How do we fall into inspiration?

The answer is, through breath, matter, and movement. That is why we do ceremonies like long dancing, drum dancing, and sun dancing. That is how I work with my students who want to progress further.

Fasting is another way to fall into inspiration. Fasting is to die into wisdom, the power, the archetype that created fasting was "to die into wisdom," or, to make whatever we thought we were disappear into wisdom. This is why we fast.

When we are drinking water, we are putting our priority on bringing light to the soul, but this is not what we want to do when we want to put all our attention toward dying. Drinking water is putting fuel into the soul, and that is the opposite of dying into wisdom. Dying into wisdom is an emptying of the soul. When we die we become the heart. We die in order to disappear into awareness.

Pʍuu-hu means to die and *pʍuu* means the heart becomes full of awareness — the kind of awareness that can now be carried by God.

We die into God when we die a physical death. We return to God, as some people say. We are already in the presence of God here, but when the spirit leaves the body, we are in a relationship with God that is different from the relationship we have with God here in the physical realm. When we are here, we have the arrogance to think we can do things ourselves.

When we are there we don't need to, because we know who God is.

Drinking light is about perception — perceptual reality. It gives us the ability to perceive things. And when we abstain from drinking light, drinking water, and just allow the darkness in the soul, that is death. By abstaining from drinking water for a while (such as during a ceremonial dance), we create a void, an emptiness into which light can come.

As soon as we get into a realm of illumination, we have left God, as we understood God prior to that moment, at that point of light. We have changed to impermanence from something permanent.

Illumination is really a point of impermanence. We only see as long as there is light to assist us to see. When we die, we go back to that infinite vastness which vibrates, but has no light. It has none of the kind of light that we use here in this state of impermanence, which has been called the *maya*, "the delusion of illusion."

In reality, there is no such thing as darkness. Here we are not talking about good and bad. In reality, the dark is neither good nor bad; it is the vibration of the breath–and the breath is inspiration.

The path of inspiration is the breath.

tehn-ku-teh
10

Sun-moon-Dance,
or OUR – G a L a x y (Na-Ku-tha-Ke) We're Dancing

Na-Ku-tha
Na-Ku-tha-Ke

moon

sun

(c) 2007
Joseph Beautiful
Painted Arrow
WA-chi-chi-Hu

appendixes

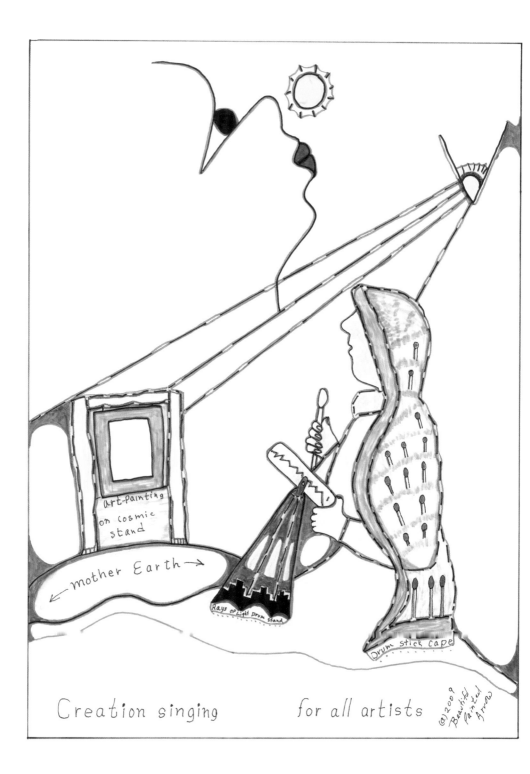

meditations and visualizations

Introduction ≈ In the audio portion of *Sound* we have recorded two different vibrations—the vibration of the Tiwa language and the vibration of the English language. Tiwa is the language that carries the vibration of the land and the English language is the language that carries the vibration of technology. Yet, whether or not you understand the Tiwa language, when you hear the language of the land you will know that language because all humanity came from sound. The language of the land is the original language of the vibration of sound.

For instance, one is pronounced "weh-hn". When you say *weh*, *weh* means life. One "*weh-hn*" means life that has just arrived. *Weh-hn*. (That "*hn*" means "just arrived.") "*Wehn*" (one) creates the cosmos.

After all, we are numbers, letters, and words, and we are the cosmos. "*Weh-mu*" is the *Tiwa* for one. Hear it? *Weh, weh, weh-mu*; *weh weh one*. The same sound is in there, very subtle. It is the same vibration.

And here is the bottom line. When I call "one" or I call "weh-mu," the same being appears. When I say "one," I see the person or being of One. I see the *Weh* Being watching us. He is in the room. And as I say the names of the other numbers, pretty soon we have a roomful of number beings sitting around here watching us, because I am calling them in.

And so you will hear the English spoken and you will understand the English that is spoken and you will also understand the language of the land. And you will hear the land singing the songs to the different levels of consciousness that we are going to present here—the consciousness of all of the numbers and the consciousness of the Being of Insight and the consciousness of all the other vibration levels.

Creation singing for all artists

233

When I call in the energies of Singing Bowl and the energies of the drum, I'm doing it with the language of the land. And because we live in the world of technology, then everything that is being recorded here includes the world of technology. So, in this book we are including the world of technology as well as the language of the land.

On the recording, we begin with the song of the calling-in of Singing Bowl and calling-in song of drum essence.

The power that is active in the drumming is *nah moh loh nay,* which means the self that is able to see the self in the deepest part of the deepest self, meaning that all of the cellular structure in the physical body is connected to going within. That is why drumming and drumming circles have been used so successfully. The very nature of *nah moh loh nay* helps that to happen. That power is in the sounds: *Nah* is the self; *moh* is to see the self; *loh* within so that the self places itself in *nay,* a statement of awareness.

josephrael.org/ drumming.mp3

Sometimes I drum with my hands and sometimes I drum with a stick, depending on what I want to achieve in the drumming. I learned to drum when I was young, with four or five other people drumming on the same big drum. They taught me to drum from the sound. They called it *nah-moh-loh-ney* and they showed me how to get in touch with the energy of *nah-moh-loh-ney* because that is the vibration of the archetype that made the original drum.

The drum is the sound of the natural world. That is why, when people journey, the drumming has helped them to achieve great success. It is in the nature of the language of the land. The world of technology may have hollowed out the cottonwood tree that we are using here and the world of technology may have tanned the hide of the drum, and

the drum stand is also made by the world of technology, but the sound that comes from the drum is the natural sound of Mother Nature.

In other words, what we are getting here is the echo. *Iii-teh-che-loh* means Echo. So when I sing "*iii-teh-che-loh*" to call in Echo, I'm calling in everything that makes up the composition of Singing Bowl. Because we need the spirit of Echo to come in and be here with us at this time to help us to vibrate. So I'm going to sing *iii-teh-che-loh.*

When I sing this song to the numbers, letters, and words, I'm going to use the Tiwa words. Remember, anything I say in Tiwa is the language of the land, and everybody knows the language of the land, even English speakers who never will hear Tiwa, because Tiwa is a language for the sake of repeating its sounds and expanding those vibrations, not so much for communication, even though people use it for communication.

Name Meditation ≈ To start the meditation on your name, find a wooden chair. It is important that you sit in that wooden chair, and you place your feet flat on the floor and your back against the chair so that you are comfortable.

Having done that, begin by relaxing all of the muscles of the body, starting with relaxing the feet muscles. After you have relaxed the feet muscles as much as you can, go up and relax the leg muscles, all the way up to the hip.

Notice that the leg muscles and the feet muscles have a connection; they are coordinated and work together, giving you the ability to walk.

In this guided meditation, we will be sometimes walking, sometimes standing, sometimes sitting and sometimes lying down and sometimes thinking and sometimes doing some kind of activity mentally.

So, if you continue relaxing the feet muscles and the leg muscles, and go on up and start relaxing all of the back muscles and the head muscles, relaxing the face muscles and the chest muscles and relaxing all of the internal organs, so that now the muscles, the hand muscles and all of the muscles of the body are relaxing.

You are taking slow deep breaths and relaxing, relaxing, relaxing. As you are relaxing, your mind is becoming more and more alert. Any sound that you are hearing is helping you to go more and more relaxed and yet your mind is becoming more and more alert. As your mind is becoming more alert, all of your body is becoming more relaxed.

Now imagine that you change your name to a verb word in vibration. In order to go into this vibration of a verb, you add the suffix 'ing' to your name. For instance, if your name is Samuel, you will add the 'ing' to the end of Samuel so that you begin to repeat the word of 'Samuel-ing,' 'Samuel-ing,' 'Samuel-ing.' Instead of 'Samuel,' you are saying 'Samuel-ing.'

Or, if your name is Mary, you will add the 'ing' to your name and become 'Mary-ing.' Do that meditation for about three minutes. During that time, play the drumming audio. At the end of those three minutes, we will go to the next step.

CHANTING – 3 minutes

Now that you find yourself in the vibration of your name, I want you to go into the vibration of the chair that you are sitting in so that both of your energies begin to blend. You are a sound vibration and the sound vibration of the wood from which the chair is made. Now the chair is the vibration of wood, so it is vibrating the 'wood-ing' energy so it is saying 'wood-ing,' 'wood-ing,' 'wood-ing,' 'wood-ing.'

josephrael.org/
chant.mp3

As you continue to repeat this sound, you will enter into that sound of 'wood-ing,' 'wood-ing,' 'wood-ing,' 'wood-ing,' 'wood-ing,' 'wood-ing.' You can, melt into the vibration of the wood because you have changed your name from a noun vibration to a verb vibration, so that you can very easily and effortlessly enter into the vibration of the chair. Imagine now, there is only a chair sitting there, and it has your vibration and you have its vibration.

So, what I want you to do now is imagine that there is this great tall beautiful being who is standing there in front of you, and (s)he is the mother/father being of all the trees that are all over the world. He is standing there, and he is there because he is interested in you because you have entered into his world of the vibration of wood. Wood is the vibration of greatness. Ask him about how keeping one's personal integrity can lead one to personal greatness.

The drumming will come on now. Stay and visit, and when the drumming ends, say goodbye to him, knowing that you can come to visit him at any time you care to do so.

Then come back and come into your body, back sitting in the chair. Once you are back in your body and sitting in the chair, count to yourself from one to five. At the count of five, you will open your eyes, you will feel good, you will feel rested, you will feel relaxed.

After this, spend at least 24 hours thinking about what you have learned because the 24 hours are also good for you to digest everything that you have experienced before you go to the next meditation.

Meditation exploring parallel realities ≈ In this song, I'm going to ask for three of the parallel realities to appear, because I want you to experience the three realities simultaneously. And you can jump from one to the other, but this time I want you to go into the song as I am singing it. I want you to go into the first reality, the second reality, and the third reality, so you get a sense of what it means to be in one, two, or three realities at the same time, because, you see, really in true life we don't exist. Because we don't exist, we can exist everywhere and nowhere at the same time. One reality will look the same as the second, parallel reality. In the first reality, for instance, you might see a drum in front of you. In the other reality, you will see the same drum, but it is going to be lying on its side. In the third reality you may see the drum floating around or something. In all three everything you see is the same except for the position of the drum.

It is just like us. Really we are not here; we are but the echo of the real us that is in a parallel reality, and what we are getting here is *maya* and *maya* is the illusion. And illusion is the most fun perception of reality because it is not real, and you create whatever you want to create, and whatever you want to create is your reality. And that is what is fun about parallel realities. I know what I'm talking about because I've been there, and I've been in them, and they're great fun.

Okay, what you do is play the drumming audio and just go into those three mirrors. After the drumming ends, you can say good-bye, knowing that you can come here to this reality anytime you want to. You give your good-byes to all of the parallel realities. Count from one to five. At the count of five, you will open your eyes. You will feel good. You will feel rested. You will feel relaxed. Wait 24 hours before you go to the next meditation.

Meditation on 1 ≈ In this next meditation, sit wherever you want to sit, in a comfortable chair or any other place where you are comfortable. Again, follow the same meditation procedure. Put both of your feet flat on the floor with your back resting against the backrest. Start relaxing all of the back muscles, the arm muscles, the leg muscles, the head muscles, the neck muscles, the face muscles, the hand muscles, all of the muscles of the body. Remember that your mind is becoming more and more alert as your body is relaxing.

josephrael.org/
drumming.mp3

After you have relaxed all the different parts of your body and your mind is now more and more alert, I want you to go through a door that is in front of you. Imagine that there is a door in front of you and you go into that door. You go into a middle room and beyond the middle room, there is another door.

As you open that door, there is a big room made out of light. Inside of this room that is made out of light, you can see above the door as you are entering, the number one. You are entering the vibration of the number one. You go into the big balloon that has the chair, and you sit on that chair. That chair has a curved back so that you are fitting in this chair almost like you would sitting in an easy chair, a very comfortable chair. It feels very comforting.

As you sit in this chair, you look in front of you and you recognize that you are inside of the vibration of number one. As you close your eyes, you begin to change your vibration from the noun vibration to the verb vibration. So your body begins to become the vibration of your name and of course the vibration of your name carries with it the vibration of your physical body, of your mental body, of your emotional and of your spiritual body. That spiritual body is responsible for giving you insights.

As you are sitting there, you begin to vibrate the vibration of your being. As you are vibrating your name vibration, you begin to vibrate and you begin to feel and sense the vibrations that are occurring. Then you begin to notice that the chair that you are sitting in is the vibration of number one. You begin to listen to the name of 'one-ing,' 'one-ing,' 'one-ing,' the vibration of number one.

'One-ing,' 'one-ing,' 'one-ing.' As you listen to the sound of 'one-ing,' 'one-ing,' you begin to feel and sense the vibration of the number one. 'One-ing,' 'one-ing,' 'one-ing,' 'one-ing,' 'one-ing,' 'one-ing,' 'one-ing,' 'one-ing' … As you begin to hear the sound of 'one-ing,' your vibration and the vibration of number one become 'one-ing,' 'one-ing,' 'one-ing,' so that now you and 'one-ing,' are one and the same. You are two different vibrations but they are two vibrations of 'one-ing,' at which point you open up your eyes in your imagination.

Even though your eyes are closed, you open up your eyes. Imagine that you see this being standing in front of you and he is in charge of the number one, of the vibration of the number one. The first thing that comes to your mind is that you want him to explain to you the vibration of what happens when you have an insight, because 'one' is the creator of insight.

He begins to explain to you what an insight means. First of all, he explains to you that an insight is an experience that you have of an inner understanding, for insight means 'to see from within.' To see within, thereby giving you an understanding of insightful things.

So, ask him to take you on a journey into the essence, into the being of insight.

The drumming will start now. Go, be with the 'number one' being, and learn.

DRUMMING – 3 minutes

josephrael.org/ drumming.mp3

visualizations and meditations

239

Say goodbye to the vibration of the one, knowing you can come back to work with the one being, and when you have finished saying your goodbyes, begin by counting to yourself from one to five. At the count of five, you will open your eyes, you will feel good, you will feel rested, you will feel relaxed as you get ready to go to the next 24 hours before your next meditation.

Meditation on 2 ≈ In this next visualization, what you do is you find a chair, you sit down comfortably, put your feet flat on the floor and you begin to relax all of the back muscles, the neck muscles, the arm muscles, the head muscles, relaxing the face muscles, relaxing the leg muscles, the feet muscles, the arm muscles, relaxing all of the muscles of the body. As you are relaxing all of the muscles of your body, your mind is going more and more alert; therefore, the mind can hear everything, understand everything that is being said and yet your mind and body are working together. They are in touch with one another, and they are working on this meditation now in which you are sitting there relaxing more and more.

As you are relaxing and going deeper and farther relaxed and your mind going more and more alert, you look in your imagination, and in front of you is a wall, and on that wall is a mirror, and you look into that mirror. You see that you are standing there. As you are looking into your image, you notice that there is a large number two that encompasses your whole body. It flashes on and then it disappears, and flashes on and disappears, and flashes on and disappears, and flashes on and disappears, and flashes on and disappears.

You realize that is an invitation for you to go into that image so that you can understand the vibrational image of the number two. You get up from where you are sitting. You walk across the room and go into your image. You fuse into that image, then you walk back and you sit in the chair. Go learn from the number two.

DRUMMING – 3 minutes

OK, now I want you to say goodbye to that presence in your body. Say goodbye to that presence of the number two in your body, knowing that you can always come back to that presence of the number two in your body. Any time you care to do so, you may do so. Begin according to the instructions I gave to count yourself back into wakefulness. Wait 24 hours until we continue this meditation again.

Meditation on 3 ≈ Find a quiet meditation place to sit down. Close your eyes as we prepare ourselves for the next meditation. As you are sitting there, as soon as you close your eyes and start taking deep breaths, very quickly your body begins to go into a meditation pose, relaxing very deeply. Farther and deeper, farther and deeper, your body goes very deep. Your mind is alert, very alert. Your mind is very alert.

In front of you is a doorway and above the doorway is the number three. So, you stand up from where you are sitting, you walk across the room and you enter the room marked three. When you get inside the room, you notice that everything is vibrating the number three sound.

It is going 'number three,' 'three,' 'three,' 'three,' 'three,' 'three,' 'three.'

Because you know the 'three' vibration, and the 'three' vibration is the sound. Remember, in the teachings, we say that the universe is made up of numbers, letters, and words. So, now you are sounding the vibration of 'three,' and you're hearing the sound vibration of 'three' because everything is molecular motion. Everything is energy. Everything is sound. Everything is letters. Everything is words.

So, you look at the wall that is in front of you and you see that there are three mirrors. There are three mirrors. In each one of these mirrors you see a picture of you looking back at you. There are three images of you in the mirrors. There is one mirror, a second mirror and a third mirror, and they

josephrael.org/
drumming.mp3

visualizations
and
meditations

241

all have an image of you. You know that you can participate in ten different parallel realities and, in this case, you will be participating in only three of them.

What you do this time is you go into the three mirrors at the same time. Now as you are entering these three images, they become landscapes so that now you find yourself as you have entered inside of the landscapes. That which was you, now change it to a landscape.

There you are, having completed entering into the part of the three aspects of your images, let one of your images visit the other two landscapes. See what you experience.

Ask your guide for guidance if you have difficulty. Play the drumming as you begin to experience the different landscapes of your being.

As the drumming ends, you can start saying your good-byes to whomever you are with. Count yourself back, as you have been doing, from one to five to wakefulness.

Again, wait twenty-four hours before doing the next meditation.

josephrael.org/
drumming.mp3

Meditation on 4 ≈ Find a comfortable chair to sit on and start taking long deep breaths. Start relaxing all of the back muscles, the neck muscles, the head muscles, the face muscles, relaxing all of the muscles of the body. As you are relaxing all of the muscles of the body, your mind is becoming more and more alert. It can hear the words that are spoken and can understand what is being said. As you are relaxing, you will notice that you are relaxing much quicker than in the other sessions because your body knows that by going deep relaxed and your mind more alert, you are able to achieve.

Because you are able to achieve mentally, emotionally, physically and spiritually, all your body then has the ability to transcend any blocks – any mental, emotional, physical, or spiritual blocks – that may be hindering your ability to go into the guided meditation.

As you are sitting there in your chair and you look on the wall, you see there is a number four above the door, so you are going into the world of number four. Imagine that you walk up to the door and you go through the door into the number four. As you go into the number four, you notice that in front of you is a beautiful summer landscape.

So, you go into the landscape of the summertime and visit there because you are the summertime now. How does it feel, for instance, to be your summertime? Enjoy meeting yourself as the summer season in the same way that Mother Nature experiences the summertime.

After you have visited there for a while, go into the autumn time, for it, too, is you. Go there and visit. See what it feels like to be Mother Nature in her autumn time and feel and sense that beingness. After you have visited your autumn time, come back and visit your wintertime and finish by visiting your springtime season.

Life is who you are, always dancing in the seasons, in the rain of spring.

josephrael.org/drumming.mp3

The drumming comes on now. Go and experience, and when the drumming ends, you will say goodbye to whomever you are with and start counting yourself to five, at which time you will open your eyes into wakefulness.

Meditation on 5 ≈ Find a quiet place, find a chair and sit down on the chair. Begin to relax all of the back muscles, the neck muscles, the head muscles, the face muscles, relaxing all of the muscles of the body. Because we have been doing these sessions, you are now able to go into deep relaxation with your mind becoming very alert very quickly.

As you are sitting there in your chair, you look up and on the wall above the door that is there is the number five. So, you get up and you walk through the door marked number five. You go into the sound vibration of the number five sound. Remember that you are the vibration of numbers, letters and words, so you can hear the sound of the word five.

Going 'five,' 'five,' 'five,' 'five,' 'five,' as a vibration ...

As you enter in the 'five' energy, imagine that in front of you is a wall with your image. So, you walk into that image of your being because, in this exercise, you will feel your physical body – how it feels and how you sense your physical body. In this exercise, also you will feel and sense your mental body. Also in this session, you will feel your emotional body so that you know how it feels and how it senses itself to you. Finally in this session, you will experience your spiritual body and how to sense and feel it, so that you can tell the difference between the way your mental body feels, your emotional body feels, your physical body feels, as well as your spiritual body.

Here you are learning about the different bodies that you represent until the drumming ends.

josephrael.org/
drumming.mp3

Meditation on 6 ≈ Find a quiet place to sit and as you sit down, you begin to relax all of the muscles of the body. Relaxing all of the back muscles, the neck muscles, the head muscles, the face muscles, the chest muscles, the leg muscles, all of the muscles of the body. Your body is going more and more relaxed, your mind becoming more and more alert. Your mind becomes alert so that it understands everything, hears everything.

At this point, we go into the number six. As you are sitting there, look at the wall and there is a door. Above the door is a number six. As you get up and walk through that door, door number six, you walk into this landscape. In this landscape you walk into, you see a tree, a big tree right in front of you, not too far away. As you walk toward that tree, you notice that everything is making a vibration. The ground is vibrating its vibrational essence. The tree is vibrating its essence.

So you want to be in tune with the tree so that you become the vibration of that beautiful tree in front of you. You walk up and you start by sliding your hand over the bark, the bark of the tree. You know that the name of that cover of the tree is called bark. The English language calls it bark, the bark of the tree. So, you start listening as you are sliding your hand down the tree with the vibration and the rhythm of bark.

"Bark," "bark," so that every time that you slide down your hand on the cover of the tree which is the bark, you hear the sound "bark," "bark," "bark." That also reminds you that there are other English words that might have this sound of "bark," "bark." For instance, if you take the 'b' away from "bark" you have "ark," "ark." And what was the Ark of the Covenant?

What other words might we compare that with? Maybe "ark," like Noah's ark? So, it reminds us of other teachings. For instance, one of the ancient mysteries is the Tree of Life. So, as you are standing there, you realize all of these special vibrations, the vibrations of teaching.

As you look to the base of the tree, you notice that your feet are on the ground and in this guided meditation, you want to get acquainted with the sound world. As you begin to step in a one-two, one-two step rhythm on the ground that you are standing on, you do it because you are remembering that one of the terms that is used in English for Mother Nature is Mother Earth.

As you go one-two, one-two, one-two, one-two with your feet, you begin to say "Mother Earth," "Mother Earth," "Mother Earth," "Mother Earth." As you begin doing that, you notice that it is true – the sound that you hear is "Mother Earth," "Mother Earth," "Mother Earth." If you want you can change that to "Mother Nature," "Mother Nature," "Mother Nature," "Mother Nature."

So it is now, you are inside and it is in you and you are outside the vibration as well of "Mother Nature" and "bark," bark of the tree, the tree vibration.

Since you have gone into the ancient sound of the tree bark and the ancient lettering (remember the Universe is made out of numbers, letters, and words), now you go to the teaching of counting. You will notice that counting also has the vibration of "one," "two," "three," "four," "five," "six," "seven,"

josephrael.org/
drumming.mp3

visualizations
and
meditations

"eight," "nine," "ten." What is one of the explanations? What do the numbers mean in some of the ancient traditions?

The numbers, in one of the ancient … very, very ancient traditions, exist to bring focus in the direction that leads to all directions. Counting, then, gives the power to manifest a great clarity, to be centered in the center of the circle of light. Counting places the heavenly planes with beauty, so that childlike innocence can prevail. So, one of the meanings of counting is so you can get in touch with the ancient mystery of the number six.

Play the drumming audio now, then after a while when the drumming ends, you will know that it is time for you to say goodbye to whomever you are with that may be assisting you in this design. Go back and get in touch with the sounds and the letters and the counting in this landscape that you find yourself in at this time.

josephrael.org/
drumming.mp3

Meditation on 7 ≈ Find a quiet place and sit in the chair. Begin to relax all of the back muscles, the neck muscles, the head muscles, the face muscles, the chest muscles, the leg muscles, relaxing all of the muscles of the body. As you are going more and more relaxed, farther and deeper, farther and deeper relaxed, your mind is becoming more and more alert. Very quickly you can go into this very deep relaxed state as you grow more alert, more relaxed. You can do this very quickly now because you have been doing these sessions for a number of times.

As you are sitting there, you look up and you see, in front of you, a wall and above that wall is a sign that says number seven and there is a doorway there. As you look closer, next to the

number seven is a description that describes number seven as "beauty of the heavens of innocence." That is because beauty is made up of all the different pathways that resonate from this vibration.

Then, as you go through the door into the being of seven, you begin to feel the vibration of seven throughout your physical body. As you go into that, you begin to start getting certain intuitions, certain thoughts. You begin to get certain understandings, certain teachings of the number seven. One of the teachings of number seven is that there are many worlds. There are many parallel realities, and they all are inside of you.

If you were the only one in the whole universe and everything else disappeared, you could make all the many worlds that exist, all the parallel realities. It is because that is who you are. So, it is, as you begin by going into one of the parallel realities. When you go into one of these parallel realities, you will see that they look exactly like the reality that you are in right now except that there are a few differences. I want you to experience those differences. Ask your guide if you have any questions on parallel realities, then go on to universes and see what they look like. Visit them and talk with the beings you will meet there in these different universes. Ask them who they are and where they belong in the cosmic essence, the cosmic vibrational order.

josephrael.org/drumming.mp3

Play the drumming audio, and hear the drumming, and when it ends, you will remember what to do. You will count yourself from one to five. At the count of five, you will open you eyes and you will sit with this number seven meditation for 24 hours before going to the next one.

Meditation on 8 ≈ Start by finding a quiet place where you sit down on the chair and you begin to relax all of the back muscles, the neck muscles, the head muscles, the face muscles, relaxing all of the muscles of the body. As you are relaxing all the muscles of the body, your mind is going more awake. Your mind understands everything, knows everything. Your body is going more and more relaxed. As you are relaxing, you can hear your breathing and your inhalations and exhalations, inhalations and exhalations, and know that that sound of the breathing is the vibration that gives you the ability to see creative intelligence at its highest potential.

You know that you are the highest creative potential and the reason is because you are the number eight, the vibration of the number eight. As you know, when you get into the vibration of the number eight (because you are vibration), linguistically, in English, you hear the word 'eight,' 'eight,' 'eight,' 'eight.' As you hear the sound, you very quickly go into the vibrancy of number eight. So, your whole physical body is vibrating the number eight. You can do this because you have just changed from a noun vibration, your name changed from a noun vibration, to a verb vibration, so you are the number eight. You have become, literally, a vibrational resonance.

So, in front of you is this picture, this picture on the wall, and it is a picture of DNA. As you look at it, you see that there are two spiraling strings. One is spiraling up, and the other is spiraling down. They are luminescent, and they are moving and they are creating tiny little vibrational essences of life. As you look at it, you realize that these strings are vibrating and these strings are connecting you to all of everything that is vibrational essence.

You can see how beautiful you are in the essence of DNA, and that you are the great clarity, the purity that carries you every day and that crystallizes the resonance of your awarenesses and all living food and all living vibration that powers your faith, that leads you to carry the heavenly planes. So, you are this vibrational resonance. As you are there watching it, you then know what you must do.

You must walk into the picture of your DNA and you walk into it because it is the size that you are. So, you get up and you walk toward that picture and you walk into the DNA.

Play the drumming audio as you explore the essence of DNA, and when the drumming ends, you will remember what to do. You will count yourself from one to five. At the count of five, you will open you eyes and you will sit with this number seven meditation for 24 hours before going to the next one.

josephrael.org/
drumming.mp3

visualizations
and
meditations

Meditation on 9 ≈ Now find a quiet place, a place where you sit down and you begin relaxing your physical body. As you are breathing and as you are relaxing, you are relaxing and breathing, and as you are doing that, you know that you are the vibrational essence of life. Relaxing all of the body muscles, relaxing all of the vibrational resonances of your being, you know that you are all of the vibrational essences that were ever created. They are in your being at this moment in time as you are relaxing all of the muscles of the body.

So, play the drumming and go on a journey to find your vibrational essence that originated your identity, which placed you in the place of belonging to being.

Knowing that you can always come back to do this practice any time you wish to do so, you can always come back to this moment, count yourself out from one to five. At the count of five, you will open your eyes, you will feel good, you will feel rested, and you will feel relaxed. You will hold this practice for 24 hours, at which time you can begin again on the next meditation.

josephrael.org/
drumming.mp3

Meditation on 10 ≈ (Steps for Collecting Sounds Meditation) First, you start this meditation by counting from one to ten, remembering that the clear pronunciation of each of the numbers from one to ten is important for collecting their true sounds. Let's just say, in this meditation, you are a sound collector of numbers.

After you finish counting the numbers from one to ten, imagine that, over to your left, there is a balloon. You take the balloon and just before you breathe into the balloon to blow it up, you breathe into your lungs the sounds of the vibrational essence of the numbers you just sounded out loud. Gather the sounds of those vibrations of those numbers from one to ten and breathe in their sounds until your lungs are full. Then get the balloon and blow into the balloon the sounds that you have just gathered.

This way you can collect the sounds from one to ten inside of the balloon. Once you have the balloon there and then you count yourself out of the meditation by counting from one to five. Once you are fully awake, you take the balloon and you let the wind out of the balloon.

As you allow the air to come out of the balloon, fix it so that the air blows on your body … covers your whole body. Now the sounds go in through your skin and now you have the sounds from one to ten in your physical body.

Next, I want you to imagine that you are looking at a tiny little granule of sand that is in front of you. It is a tiny little granule of sand, and you look at it. Imagine yourself getting smaller and smaller and smaller until you have gotten so very small that you can walk into that tiny little granule of sand.

Once you get into that little granule of sand, I want you to imagine that you become even smaller, only this time you and the sand granule together become smaller and smaller until you are three trillion times smaller. When you reach that level imagine that, in front of you, there is a door and you go through that door.

Beyond the door is a swimming pool. In that swimming pool, the water is made up of all of the archetypes and all of the principal ideas that make up the consciousness of the cosmos. Imagine yourself walking into that pool of light. Inside that pool of light you immerse yourself, as you go down and dive into that beautiful light. You come up out of that pool of light and you go back through the door.

You sit inside that tiny little granule of sand. Then imagine yourself coming back, getting bigger and farther and bigger and you come back and back until finally you decide that you are now sitting in your meditation chair.

Now you are ready to go out into the world because you have the numbers in words to carry you always.

the stages of growth into consciousness

When we are born, we are born raw, and as we progress in life we get more "cooked" until eventually we are well done. We come unmarked and unformed, and we grow into perception through experience.

There are several levels of maturation that are required by Mother Nature for us to experience as we grow into women or men. They can be said to be stages of growth into consciousness. These are steps that women and men must go through, not simply because they are women or men. In each individual, the feminine or masculine needs to be born and nurtured so that that particular aspect of consciousness can grow.

The feminine is that aspect of life that is constantly in a state of flow. It is like descending light that can never stop without the masculine aspect. The masculine is that aspect of life that stops or tries to stop the flow in persons, places or things. The masculine is the aspect that falls from grace, because the flow is grace. Technology becomes possible with the masculine aspect.

When we learn, we work with three levels of energy: intellect, the intuitive, and the spiritual. The intellectual level involves the *maa* energy. We analyze, we take notes, we memorize. The intuitive level bypasses all this action of the intellect. It involves the *waa* energy. The spiritual involves *chi* energy, which is a higher vibration still.

Life is made out of a chain of events somehow similar to the unfolding of a normal day and night. Your day (or your life) might unfold somewhat like this example:

Step 1: You awake out of physical sleep

Step 2: You wash, shower, and get dressed

Step 3: You eat breakfast

Step 4: You prepare to go to the office

Step 5: You travel to work

Step 6: You're at work when a phone call comes and stops the flow of the morning's events. The call is disruptive. It is the masculine at work. You stop the flow in order to start a different movement.

Remember that there is really no "up-and-down" continuum, but that we create these metaphors here in order to give purity, placement, awareness, innocence, and carrying a structure. Only when these are ordered in a structure can we perceive that which cannot be seen. After all is said and done, we are simply being and vibration.

Here are the stages of life (developing feminine energy) and their Tiwa names:

1. *Oh-tie*—fetus in the womb

2. *Oh-see-aah- who*—baby in the act of birthing

3. *Oh-see-aah-ii*—the moment at which the child takes its first breath

4. *Oh-chi-ack-key-aah-oh-nay*—infant (0 to 5 years old)

5. *Oh-oh-peeh-yo-nay*—little girl (5 to 6 years old)
   Oh-cho-oh-nay—little boy (5 to 6 years old)

6. *Oh-peh-yo-nay*—girl (6 to 14 years old)
   Oh-cho-nay—boy (6 to 14 years old)

7. *Oh-peh-yo-quol-ley-nay*—girl 14 to 16 years old
   Oh-cho-co-queh-nay—boy 14 to 16 years old

8. *Quol-ley-nay*—girl 16 to 20 years old
   Co-queh-nay—boy 16 to 20 years old

9. *Quol-lee-hue-way-nay*—woman 20 to 25 years old
   Co-queh-sue-may-nay—man 20 to 25 years old

10. *Lee-hue-way-nay*—woman 25 to 55 years old
    Sue-may-nay—man 25 to 55 years old

11. *Key-ah-tah-meh-nay*—Elder (55 to 75 years old) (It is only after he or she reaches this stage that a person can officially become a storyteller.)

12. *Lee-hue-lah-oh-nay*—Old woman (75 + years old)
    Sol-thay-own-nay—Old man (75 + years old)

Step 1: Both the feminine and the masculine are teaching the baby. *Oh-tie* is teaching during the different embryonic stages inside the womb. *Oh-tie* teaches the child to be open to learning as a forward and backward motion—to be open to learning by doing.

Step 2: When the child is in the birthing process (vaginal canal), she is at the stage of *oh-see-aah-who*. *Oh-see-aah-who* teaches to be open to learning how placement purifies through polarity or struggle. Learning is infused into the psyche through struggle or polarity in order to move towards reconciliation, spiritual purpose, and transformational potential.

Step 3: *Oh-see-aah-ii*, or the point where the child takes its first breath, is teaching the child how struggle or polarity invites awareness as self-identity. Before it takes its first breath, the child does not exist. Then the child breathes and it has an individual identity of breath, matter, and movement.

Step 4: *Oh-chi-aah-key-aah-oh-nay* says that teachability comes through movement. Motion is the same as perceivable reality. Motion teaches while it purifies the personal self and connects all teachings to the Vast Self as well. *Tu-caa*, which means purifying, is the vibration that cleanses and sanctifies that which is learned. Now it can be seen as a body of beauty made of universal intelligence.

Step 5: *Oh-oh-peeh-yo-oh-nay.* At this stage the child is learning to reflect upon what it sees. On the feminine side, this reflection connects the spiritual body (that which inspires) with the heart body (that which feels). On the masculine side, the child is learning divine movement and how the psyche is always open to the learning which may be available internally or externally, from mental, emotional, physical, or spiritual bodies.

Step 6: *Oh-peeh-yo-oh-nay* on the feminine side teaches how to connect seeing (*pee-yo*) with curiosity as receptivity. On the masculine side, meanwhile, the girl is learning to climb upward to find the beauty of new self-discovery. She climbs up in order to connect to the Vast Self. In her individuality, that Vast Self is grounded. In Tiwa thought, nothing exists unless it is grounded, unless it is based on the divine longing to exist.

Step 7: *Oh-peh-yo-quol-ley-nay* on the feminine side teaches the girl to bring separateness into her oneness, to become an individual. On the masculine side, she is learning that beauty and standing are the same, and standing means existing in oneness, as an individual.

Step 8: Here the girl or boy continues the lessons of *oh-peh-yo-quol-ley-nay* that were begun in the step above.

Step 9: This period of life teaches the person on the feminine side to continue to be receptive to new insights in order to keep renewing beauty. The masculine is teaching that beauty and standing existence must be substantiated by a spiritual life and death in order for renewal to occur. (Life is now seen not as a continuum so much as a series of deaths and rebirths through which the person's individual beauty is continually being renewed.)

Step 10: The feminine teaches the person that descending light comes bringing insight. The masculine teaches that divine longing is necessary for the person to move upward toward purity.

Step 11: The feminine teaches "mother-ness," or receptivity. The masculine teaches "father-ness," or activity. These two teachings combine as the Mother-Father-God principle. *Key-aah-ta-meh-nay* women and men are elders in the community. At this stage, they are considered well-done, well cooked, and can now teach the traditions because they have passed all the stages successfully and have acquired a deep understanding of "metaphor alongside experience."

Step 12: In old age, the feminine teaches that wisdom descends from above, while the masculine teaches that which falls from above is full of ancient wisdom, which can only be used or understood after it has been grounded on the physical plane.

links to joseph's audio streams online:

about sound and ceremony

josephrael.org/bmm.mp3

josephrael.org/singtobowl.mp3

josephrael.org/beginning.mp3

josephrael.org/effort.mp3

joscphrael.org/dances.mp3

josephrael.org/light.mp3

josephrael.org/land.mp3

josephrael.org/expand.mp3

josephrael.org/fasting.mp3

josephrael.org/break.mp3

josephrael.org/breath.mp3

josephrael.org/origins.mp3

josephrael.org/reconcile.mp3

josephrael.org/music.mp3

josephrael.org/origins.mp3

josephrael.org/nature.mp3

vowel sounds and their esoteric meanings

josephrael.org/AEIOU.mp3

josephrael.org/ahhh.mp3

josephrael.org/ehh.mp3

josephrael.org/ohh.mp3

josephrael.org/iii.mp3

josephrael.org/uuu.mp3

numbers 1 through 10 in Tiwa

josephrael.org/1weh-mu.mp3

josephrael.org/2weh-seh.mp3

josephrael.org/3pah-chu.mp3

josephrael.org/4wiii.mp3

josephrael.org/5pah-nu.mp3

josephrael.org/6mah-tschlay.mp3

josephrael.org/7cho-oh.mp3

josephrael.org/8wheh-leh.mp3

josephrael.org/9whiii.mp3

josephrael.org/10tehn-ku-teh.mp3

chanting and drumming

josephrael.org/drumming.mp3

josephrael.org/chant.mp3

message to the elders

josephrael.org/elders.mp3

message to the elders

I believe that it is now time for the elders all over the world to talk to their people and instruct them. As elders we have more responsibility ... a responsibility to talk about the sacredness of the Earth, and the sacredness of the people on the Earth. One of our journeys is to help the people as they walk on Mother Earth. Mother Earth is our land and she belongs to us because we are her children. She belongs to us and we belong to her. So we can take care of her the way she has been taking care of us.

As elders we can tell our people that now is the time to do this. We have a responsibility as elders to live so that generations that follow us will continue the work of living with Mother Earth so that Mother Earth will bless us in the way she has blessed us in the past.

josephrael.org/
elders.mp3

We are now reaching our autumn time, and in our autumn time we elders have a responsibility because soon we will be going beyond our wintertime. Our seasons of the spring and summer have passed. As we leave, we can leave our children's children's children a message of hope and light. That message will be that in the end we are all brothers and sisters, mothers and fathers, uncles and aunts, extended families, and we belong to one great Mystery, the Mystery that created us in the beginning.

And this is the message I present at this time to all of the elders and all of the mystics and others who also belong to the first circle of light, which made it possible for all of us, all different tribes, all different peoples, to come to this dance, this singing, this Long Dance of life.

A-Ho!

JOSEPH RAEL, 2009